Everyday Adventures

50 new ways to experience your hometown

Everyday

dventures

Contents

Introduction

ADVENTURE IS A WAY OF LIFE

You don't need to travel far to see the world with fresh eyes. It was on a drizzly day in London, clutching my camera, that I learned to love my home city again.

After years of weaving through crowds and avoiding eye contact in train compartments, my love affair with London felt rocky. Then, on a short photography course, my teacher urged me to zoom in on London's hidden beauty. Through a lens, I saw my surroundings anew. At ground level, candy-coloured high-heeled shoes struck the pavement with haughty, rhythmic steps. Corrugated iron, Victorian-style windows, the frayed spines of volumes in a second-hand book shop...textures and shapes I'd usually ignore looked fascinating through a camera.

The art of macro photography (p.22) is one of 50 bite-sized escapades in this book. These 'everyday adventures' are designed to revitalise your relationship with your corner of the world. And you don't need to spend big or travel far: transform your commute into a holiday (p.122), tap into your subconscious mind on a suburban stroll (p.46), or escape from reality in your own backyard (p.57).

So what kind of adventure suits your mood? Our 'Challenge Yourself' chapter has 10 ways to test your boundaries. 'Cultural Odysseys' is packed with forays into local history and art. In 'Follow Your Senses' you can sniff, listen and eat your way to new insights. 'Roll the Dice' flings you out of your rut with games to guide your way. Finally, in 'Social Adventures', you can bring family and friends along for the ride.

It's time to weave some wonderment into your daily routine.

HAPPY ADVENTURING,
ANITA ISALSKA, EDITOR

PICCADILL

5

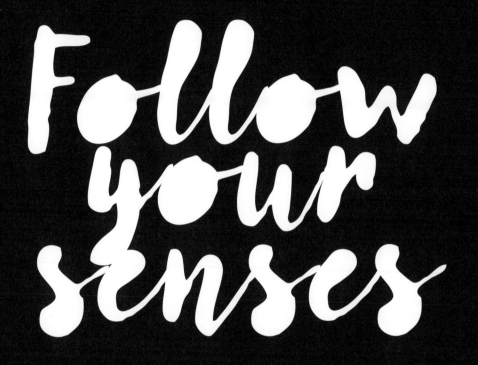

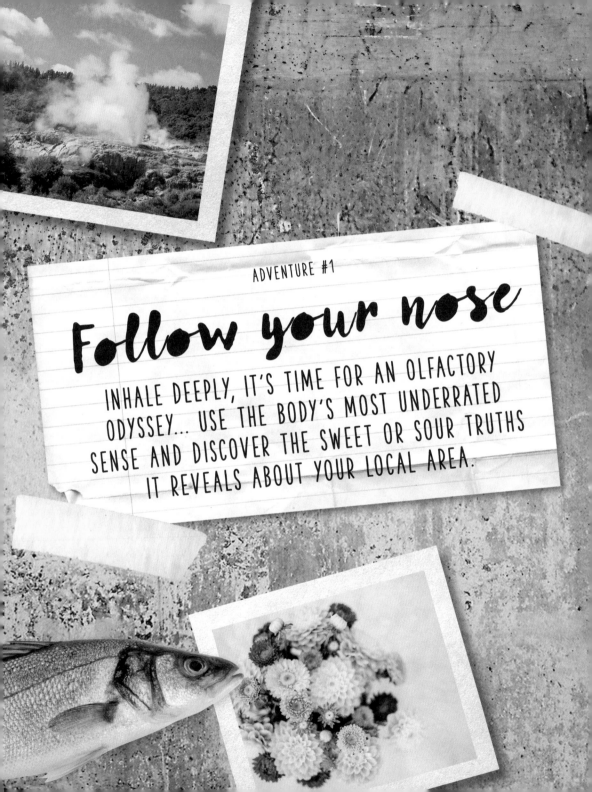

ADVENTURE #1

Follow your nose

INHALE DEEPLY, IT'S TIME FOR AN OLFACTORY ODYSSEY... USE THE BODY'S MOST UNDERRATED SENSE AND DISCOVER THE SWEET OR SOUR TRUTHS IT REVEALS ABOUT YOUR LOCAL AREA.

What you'll need

AN AREA REPLETE WITH INTRIGUING ODOURS

Instructions

1. PICK A SUITABLY SMELLY STARTING POINT: IT COULD BE A FISH MARKET, BAKERY OR A FLOWER-FILLED PARK.

2. BREATHE IN, AND LET THE STRONGEST SMELL IN YOUR VICINITY ENVELOP YOU. IS IT APPETISING, INTRIGUING OR (BETTER YET) EYE-WATERINGLY RANCID? WALK OR CYCLE TO ITS SOURCE.

3. YOUR NEWLY ENERGISED NOSTRILS SHOULD BE PICKING UP ON ALL SORTS OF ODOURS BY NOW, SO SNIFF A SECOND SMELL AND WALK IN ITS DIRECTION.

4. DON'T SMELL ANYTHING? WALK OR CYCLE AWAY FROM THE ORBIT OF YOUR STARTER STINK UNTIL SOMETHING NEW TICKLES YOUR NOSE.

COMPLEXITY ★ ★ ★ ★ ★

Case study
Virginia Jealous, Scentsitive Cyclist

In Denmark, on the far south coast of Western Australia, we live life on the edge: edge of river, inlet, ocean and continent. The bicycle route from town to the wild Southern Ocean hugs this fringe and is landmarked by smells both marvellous and malodorous. A cycle ride gives my nose, and my legs, a surprisingly good workout.

A perfect morning smell starts the day, wafting from the riverside coffee roaster. Inhaling is *almost* as good as imbibing but not quite, so I stop for a caffeine hit.

Shops begin to open. A smoky haze of incense from the fair-trade store really gets up my nose. I pause – upwind – to watch the responses of other passersby. These vary from 'ooh, lovely' to sneezing and nose-blowing. Pushing my bike along the main street I take time out to smell the roses by the war memorial, and to talk plants with the council gardeners who are spreading blood-and-bone manure on the flowerbeds.

Downstream a couple of kilometres, where river meets inlet, the sharp smell of bird poo make me slow down and look up. Silhouetted against sky, the roosts and nests of cormorants are visible in the tree tops. Mornings and evenings are punctuated by the flap and clatter of thousands of wings as they leave and return in noisy flocks.

The clean salt air of the ocean beckons me on. In summer, beachside bushland is pungent with the smell of eucalyptus. In winter, smoke from bonfires infiltrates my clothes. It's a scented souvenir that lingers long after getting home.

Pros and Cons

+ Blooming plants and blooming friendships
- Unappetising pongs

Scent of Survival

Your nostrils are portals to your evolutionary history. Humankind honed its sense of smell back when a whiff of rotten food helped avoid sickness, or reeking body odour signalled an impending fight. A study published in *Science* declared that the average person can detect one trillion different odours. The region of the brain responsible for detecting odours, the olfactory bulb, is larger in humans than in most mammals. Given the link between our sense of smell and the amygdala and hippocampus – areas of the brain tied to emotion – odours guide our decision-making in subtle ways. Whether it's fresh doughnuts or petrol fumes, scent triggers mood changes. Inability to discern between smells is even considered an early warning sign of Alzheimer's disease.

FRESHLY BAKED BREAD
IS ONE OF A TRILLION
ODOURS DETECTABLE BY
YOUR HUMBLE HOOTER

urban foraging

AFTER A DAY OF FORAGING, YOU'LL HAVE MORE THAN A BAG BRIMMING WITH PRODUCE – YOUR BRAIN WILL BULGE WITH KNOWLEDGE ABOUT YOUR LOCAL GREEN SPACES.

What you'll need

AN EXPERT BOTANICAL EYE (YOURS OR A GUIDE'S)

Instructions

FORAGING ISN'T ONLY FOR COUNTRY-DWELLERS. BERRIES AND MUSHROOMS PEEP OUT BETWEEN APARTMENT BLOCKS AND VEGETABLES GROW IN URBAN PARKLAND.

FERRET AROUND IN UNTAMED GRASSLANDS, RATHER THAN MANICURED PARKS, AND ALWAYS FORAGE FAR FROM PATHWAYS (WHERE DOG PEE OR PESTICIDES MIGHT BE SPRINKLED). LEAVE ROOTS UN-TUGGED AND DON'T TAKE MORE THAN YOU'LL EAT.

TO THE UNTRAINED EYE, THE SHAPE OF A LEAF CAN BE THE DIFFERENCE BETWEEN A HAND-PICKED SALAD AND A NIGHT SPENT IN THE EMERGENCY ROOM (OR WORSE). START FORAGING ON A GUIDED TOUR LED BY A BOTANY PRO.

COMPLEXITY ★ ★ ★ ★ ★

Case study

Lorna Parkes,
Leeds-Based Food-Lover

People think you have to be in the wild to find edible plants and fungi, but the urban environment can be just as bountiful a larder if you know what you're looking at. Behind an industrial estate bordering one of the main arteries in Leeds, England, I'm wading through a wasteland of unruly grasses with Lisa Cutcliffe, who runs Edulis Wild Food from her city terrace house. We're here to track down ruby-red wild plums that glint like jewels from the road. Even this close to traffic, anything with a shiny skin that can be washed and scrubbed is fair game for the urban forager.

The evensong of an ice-cream van signals an opportunistic worker doing rounds of back-to-back terraces at the end of the field. The van's tinny tinkle, accompanied by the drone of cars, bird twitter and dog walkers' chitter chatter, make for an eclectic urban orchestra at dusk. Dinner calls: we load up with wild plums for a duck sauce and bitter-orange hogweed seeds for seasoning, then move on.

Our next stop is a sprawling inner-city park. Children play in the fading light and windows glow as lights are switched on by workers returning home. The feather-soft coo of a wood pigeon drifts on the air as we move deeper into the park.

Shamrock-shaped wood sorrel – 'nature's sherbet', Lisa enthuses – makes it into the basket for a zingy salad. Trees are scoured for sulphur-coloured eruptions of Chicken of the Woods mushrooms, and we hunt hopefully for the last of the season's wild garlic leaves. We hear our final stop before we see it: a Linden tree humming with bees, the blossoms from which will be mashed for a floral tea. Tonight, our feast is on the city.

Pros and Cons

+ Bulging basket of produce
- Nettle stings and mud stains

End Times Survival

Planning ahead to nuclear meltdown or the zombie apocalypse? Urban foraging is your first step towards self-sufficiency – but it's a heck of a steep learning curve. Journalist Becky Lerner documented foraging in her native Portland, Oregon in her book *Dandelion Hunter*. There are highs, lows and hunger pangs, especially when Lerner attempts to live on foraged produce alone.

Occupying a much more extreme end of the self-sufficiency spectrum is society refusenik Chris McCandless, who ventured into the Alaskan wilds hoping to survive on what he foraged and hunted. McCandless' death – widely believed to be the result of starvation – reached mythic status following a biography and movie about his life, both titled *Into The Wild*.

MAKE A NOTE OF WHERE YOU FIND THE BEST FORAGED GOODIES SO YOU CAN HUNT THEM OUT AGAIN NEXT SEASON

Fly by night

SUBMIT TO THE DARK SIDE AND GAIN A NOCTURNAL PERSPECTIVE ON YOUR NEIGHBOURHOOD...

What you'll need

FLASHLIGHT

BASIC SAFETY PRECAUTIONS

NERVES OF STEEL

Instructions

CITIES ARE DIFFERENT AFTER DARK: MERRY MARKETPLACES BECOME EERIE, GARDENS HUM WITH A STRANGE, NOCTURNAL SOUNDTRACK, AND FAMILIAR LANDMARKS BECOME UNRECOGNISABLE.

START IN YOUR OWN BACKYARD: HOW ARE ITS SIGHTS AND SOUNDS DIFFERENT AFTER MIDNIGHT? EMBOLDENED, VENTURE ON TO YOUR HIGH STREET, FAVOURITE PARK, ANYWHERE YOU KNOW WELL BUT HAVE NEVER SEEN AFTER SUNDOWN.

CHOOSE YOUR LOCATION WISELY AND DON'T EMBARK ON THIS ADVENTURE ALONE...

COMPLEXITY ✷ ✷ ✩ ✩ ✩

Case study
John A. Vlahides, Nocturnal Explorer

The tiny town of Boulder, Utah (population 180) spreads out along a verdant valley, a peaceful oasis in an otherwise forbidding landscape. I arrive at twilight and see that there are just a few houses, a motel, several shops, a restaurant and a cafe along Boulder's mile-long main drag.

At around 10pm I set out to explore. Southern Utah's night sky is jam-packed with a million twinkling stars. I walk along the double-yellow line of deserted Main St, my footsteps the only sound. Except for a couple of streetlights, everything is in darkness.

I saunter to the town hall, where I cup my hands on the glass to see inside. Nothing. I do the same at a curio shop and the Mormon temple. Can't see a thing. Provoked by my noisy footsteps, a dog barks viciously. Adrenaline courses through my veins. I hold my breath and look for the animal, but can't see into the blackness.

I suddenly feel less like an adventurer and more like a target for some ruffian, wild animal, ghost. It occurs to me that I may not be alone. I've been ambling along, talking to myself, peering into windows, not even bothering to look over my shoulder.

Back in my motel, I turn off the light and stare out at the stars. The constellations are all that's worth seeing in Boulder tonight. As for the rest, I'll check it out tomorrow, when the dogs and ghosts retreat from the searing noonday sun.

Pros and Cons

+ Starry skies
+ Majestic silence
- Horror-movie flashbacks

ADVENTURE #4

Macro lensing

ZOOM IN ON LESSER-OBSERVED BEAUTY
WITH THE HELP OF A MACRO LENS.

What you'll need

CAMERA

Instructions

1. IT'S BEST TO HAVE AN SLR CAMERA AND MACRO LENS - BUT YOU CAN TRY THIS ADVENTURE WITH ANY CAMERA GOOD ENOUGH TO ZOOM.

2. PHOTOGRAPHY WITH A MACRO LENS CREATES IMAGES THAT ARE LARGER THAN THE SUBJECT ITSELF. IF YOU HAVE A BASIC DIGITAL COMPACT CAMERA, SIMPLY ENGAGE 'MACRO' MODE AND ZOOM IN.

3. YOUR CHALLENGE IS TO REVEAL THE BEAUTY IN EVERYDAY LOCATIONS. YOU COULD PHOTOGRAPH COFFEE FOAM, PAVING STONES, EVEN MOULD SPLOTCHES. IF CAPTURING WATER-LADEN LEAVES AND GRASS, GO JUST AFTER RAINFALL. ALTERNATIVELY, HEAD OUT IN EARLY EVENING FOR THE 'GOLDEN HOUR'.

COMPLEXITY ★ ★ ★ ★ ☆

23

Case study

Kerry Christiani, Nature Observer & Photographer

A macro lens is like a window to another world. Pop one onto your SLR camera and suddenly it's as though you've been admitted to a secret society – at eye level with the emerging buds and nectar-sapping bees, the undergrowth and cracked mud. Zooming in on nature this way makes the mundane seem magical.

Since starting to explore my surrounding environment with a macro lens, I'll never look at a leaf, fern, rock or frozen puddle in quite the same way again. The patterns that emerge with shallow depth of field are astonishing: the filigree fronds of a plant, the abstract patterning and micro air bubbles in ice, the silken folds of a peony in bloom.

Macro photography is about making the ordinary appear extraordinary; about seeing the familiar with new eyes and newfound wonder. I now notice art in nature wherever I look in Wales, be it in the reflection of tree branches in a flooded wood in Carmarthenshire, the cerulean swirls of eddies on the Pembrokeshire coast, or moors and buttercup-freckled meadows drenched in the golden light of spring in the Brecons.

Even on the drabbest days of the long Welsh winter, the macro lens inspires me to get out and get creative. Grey weather can work in favour of the still-life photographer. There are cobwebs hung heavy with fat raindrops, barbed wire entangled with sheep's wool, and dripping, filamentous lichens to capture on camera. Such beauty is all around us, if only we open our eyes (and lenses) to see it.

Pros and Cons

+ Abstract photos
- Expensive camera kit

Paranormal Pics

Ever since photographic technology became widespread, photographers have devised techniques to create fake images. William H Mumler has the dubious acclaim of being the world's first 'spirit photographer'. The 19th-century photographer doctored images to create ghostly hands resting on his subjects' shoulders. Mumler built a lucrative business, capitalising on the grief of families who lost loved ones in the American Civil War; many of his photographs show long-dead loved ones embracing their living relatives. This cynical ploy was eventually exposed, along with charges that Mumler broke into houses to steal photos with which to doctor his images. Public disgrace followed; but photographers have continued faking paranormal photos for centuries since.

FAMILIAR TEXTURES
ASSUME AN ALIEN
QUALITY UNDER A MACRO
LENS. GET YOUR FRIENDS
TO GUESS WHAT YOU'VE
PHOTOGRAPHED

25

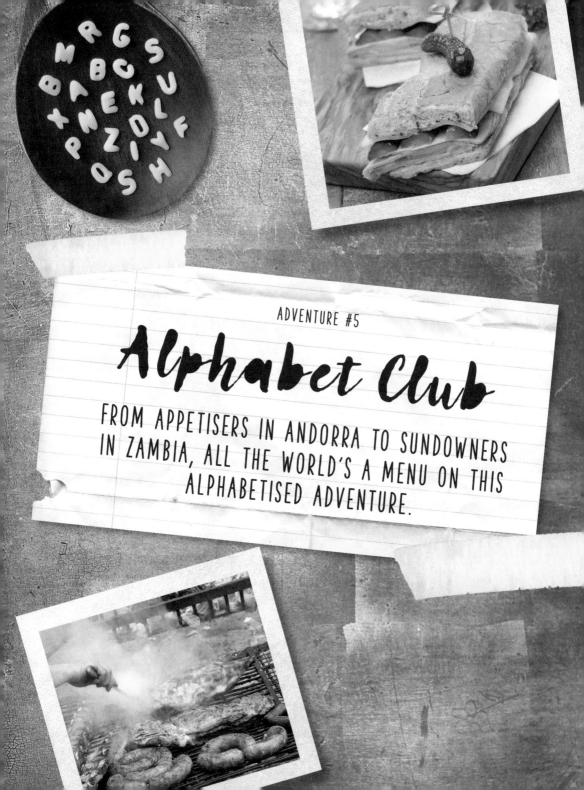

Alphabet Club

FROM APPETISERS IN ANDORRA TO SUNDOWNERS IN ZAMBIA, ALL THE WORLD'S A MENU ON THIS ALPHABETISED ADVENTURE.

What you'll need

HUNGRY FRIENDS

ELASTICATED WAISTBAND

Instructions

1. YOUR MISSION IS TO TACKLE AS MANY WORLD CUISINES AS YOU CAN, WEEK BY WEEK, IN ALPHABETICAL ORDER BY COUNTRY.

2. START BY SEEKING OUT A CAFE OR RESTAURANT SERVING AUSTRIAN, ARGENTINIAN, ALBANIAN OR ANY OTHER CUISINE BEGINNING WITH 'A'. NEXT MOVE ON TO 'B' FOR BRAZILIAN, BELGIAN OR BANGLADESHI. SEE HOW FAR YOU CAN GET THROUGH THE ALPHABET.

3. WHERE YOU HAVE A CHOICE OF CUISINES, CHOOSE THE ONE THAT THE FEWEST PEOPLE IN YOUR GROUP HAVE TRIED (WE'D PICK SERBIAN OVER SPANISH).

COMPLEXITY ★ ★ ★ ☆ ☆

Case study
Lauren Keith, Eater-in-Chief

You've heard it before: London is a global city, capital of the world. But could I eat my way through the whole world without going to the airport?

I decided to go through the world's countries in alphabetical order and feast in a London restaurant for each one. I couldn't find an Andorran restaurant, so I decided to make the national dish at home...until I saw that I'd have to procure skinned chicken feet, lamb ankles and two pounds of bones and marrow. Sorry, Andorra. Then I contacted the Angolan embassy for suggestions, to no reply. Surely there's a consular branch for that?

Friends suggested I choose *one* country for each letter of the alphabet. Hunting down cuisines took my friends and I into all corners of the city. Who knew a concentration of Lithuanian restaurants existed in Leyton or that you could get a banana-leaf-wrapped Cambodian meal in Camden? The world was my Oyster card.

Failing to find an Omani restaurant we went with Österreich (German for Austria), eating schnitzel in a kitsched-out *bierkeller* while the 80-year-old, lederhosen-wearing owner put on his nightly 'cowbell show'. Scouring the web didn't reveal Qatari restaurants so we toasted London with breakfast on the 31st floor of the Qatari-owned Shard skyscraper.

Soon we'll make it to Z, but the adventures won't stop there. We'll start another trip around London, around the world.

Pros and Cons

+ Expanding culinary horizons
− Expanding waistline

CAN'T FIND A RESTAURANT
FOR EVERY LETTER? PICK A
COUNTRY'S NATIONAL DISH AND
MAKE IT AT HOME

Acquired Tastes

Munching your way through the world, you'll inevitably discover gastronomy you *aren't* keen on – whether it's bird foetus boiled in its own egg (the Philippines) or *hákarl*, whiffy cured shark (Iceland). Top of the daredevil menu is Greenlandic *kiviak*. To Inuit people, it's a staple for surviving brutally cold winters; to untrained palates, it's so pungent that even daring foodies will feign loss of appetite. To make kiviak, a few dozen auks (seabirds) are stuffed into a hollowed-out seal carcass. The sealskin is sewed up, sealed with fat for good measure, then buried beneath a pile of rocks. Months later, kiviak is ready to eat: feathers are easy to peel away, bones have softened during fermentation, and there's plenty of fatty meat to chew on through winter.

ADVENTURE #6

Count the birds

WITH THIS DECEPTIVELY SIMPLE EXERCISE, COUNT FEATHERED FRIENDS TO ACHIEVE HEIGHTENED MINDFULNESS.

What you'll need

A TREE-LINED PLACE TO SIT
ORNITHOLOGICAL KNOWLEDGE (OPTIONAL)

Instructions

HOW MUCH NATURE SURROUNDS YOU, EVEN IN THE MIDST OF A CITY? SEE WHAT YOU DISCOVER WHEN YOU PAUSE AND TAKE STOCK OF THE WILDLIFE AROUND YOU, IN THIS CASE BY SIMPLY COUNTING BIRDS.

ON A DRY-WEATHER DAY, FIND A COMFY PLACE TO SIT OUTSIDE: A LAWN, PARK BENCH OR ANY TRANQUIL OUTDOOR SPOT WILL DO. TUNE YOUR EARS TO THE SOUND OF BIRDSONG. HOW MANY BIRDS CAN YOU COUNT IN THE SPACE OF AN HOUR? WHAT SPECIES DO YOU SEE, WHAT SONGS DO YOU HEAR? AND WHAT ELSE IS CONTRIBUTING TO THE SOUNDTRACK: LEAVES CARRIED ON THE BREEZE, HUMMING INSECTS, OR JUST YOUR NEIGHBOURS' QUESTIONABLE TASTE IN MUSIC?

COMPLEXITY ★ ★ ★ ★ ★

Case study
Karyn Noble, Hayfeverish Bird Lover

London, 6pm, 28°C. Pollen count: very high. I'm sitting on the sun-warmed wooden seat in my garden for the first time. No, I've not just moved in. I've lived here *over a year*. I wiggle my toes on the cool grass as I wait, with pen and notebook, for all the birds I'll count.

Three minutes in and a buzzing sound captures my attention. One big bumblebee in a white flower. Another near a red flower. After several more minutes – effortlessly – the names of these flowers abruptly pop into my head: snapdragon and geranium. Is this going to be a byproduct of my hour in the garden? Noticeable brain improvement? I'm quietly impressed. Further senses are awakening: I smell the geraniums and also a waft of lavender from the other side of the garden path. And the coals of someone's barbecue.

Two magpies fly overhead, a reminder I need to be looking up as well as down and around. Twenty minutes in and a blackbird trusts my stillness to land on the grass. Three minutes later there's a gentle flutter in the shrubs and a robin appears! I don't dare breathe. Yet out of the corner of my eye I see my neighbour Eddie opening the garden gate to my right. Nooooooo! I keep my gaze fixated on the robin.

'Nice and quiet,' Eddie says. I whisper 'yes' with a smile, before looking back to the robin.

'Enjoying the birdlife,' Eddie purrs, like he's narrating a David Attenborough documentary, and disappears. Disappointingly, so does the robin. All up I spot 35 birds and my hayfeverish sneezes don't start until 55 minutes in. That definitely counts for something.

Pros and Cons

✚ Fresh air and trilling birdsong
− Neighbours like Eddie

THERE ARE AN ESTIMATED
18,000 DIFFERENT BIRD SPECIES
IN THE WORLD, NOT ALL OF
THEM YET DISCOVERED

Feathery Doom-Bringers

When counting birds, it's handy to know their species – indeed, your fate may depend on it. If you've ever heard the rhyme 'one for sorrow, two for joy' about magpies, you've already participated in the long tradition of predicting the future through birds. Eagles represented nobility in cultures from Native American to Aztec. Owls were once considered to be a favoured bird of the goddess Athena but their nocturnal hooting later became associated with imminent disaster. Since Samuel Taylor Coleridge wrote *The Rime of the Ancient Mariner* (1798), the albatross has become associated with psychological torment – fortunately you're unlikely to spot this cursed seabird from your garden.

COUNT BIRDS IN A PLACE
YOU WON'T BE DISTURBED,
TO AVOID ANY HAWKWARD
MOMENTS

ADVENTURE #7

Food Quest

HUNT DOWN THE FOOD SOURCES AND FRIENDLY FACES BEHIND YOUR WEEKLY SHOP.

What you'll need

APPETITE FOR LOCAL PRODUCE

BIKE OR CAR

Instructions

GAIN A RENEWED APPRECIATION FOR WHAT YOU EAT BY FINDING YOUR LOCAL FOOD SOURCES. IF YOU ALREADY HAVE FAVOURITE LOCALLY GROWN FOODS, WHETHER CHEESES OR JAMS OR VEGGIES, YOUR QUEST IS TO TRACE BACK TO THEIR SOURCE. IF NOTHING IN PARTICULAR SPRINGS TO MIND, BEGIN AT THE NEAREST FARMERS' MARKET FOR INSPIRATION.

INVESTIGATING LOCAL FOOD SOURCES WON'T NECESSARILY MAKE YOU FEEL WARM AND FUZZY. FOR EVERY STRAWBERRY FARM HUMMING WITH BEES, YOU RISK ENCOUNTERING A GRIM FACTORY. TRY TO TREAT GOOD AND BAD DISCOVERIES AS PART OF THE PATH TO UNDERSTANDING FOOD'S JOURNEY TO YOUR TABLE.

COMPLEXITY ★ ★ ★ ★ ✳

35

Case study
Carolyn B. Heller, Omnivorous Eater

The farmers' market in downtown Vancouver is my calendar. Greens and strawberries mean spring. Plums arrive with autumn. Inspired by the market, I decide to learn more.

I pedal my bike west toward UBC Farm, where local students cultivate carrots, berries, even hops for a local microbrewery. I learn that the farm has partnered with the Musqueam First Nation, whose territory encompasses much of present-day Vancouver, to grow yarrow, lavender, and medicinal plants in traditional curved beds.

The next weekend, my husband Alan and I cycle along the West Dyke Trail to Steveston, an active fishing port. We visit the Gulf of Georgia Cannery, the largest of 15 fish processing facilities that once lined the waterfront, glimpsing into the lives of immigrant and First Nations workers who staffed the canning lines. Alan eyes a whole fish, before deciding not to pedal home with seven kilos of tuna sticking out of his backpack.

It's a sunny Sunday when my daughter Talia and I drive over a single-lane wooden bridge to pick strawberries on a Westham Island farm. It's hard work, squatting between plants and hunting for ruby-red fruits. In an hour, we're surprised to discover that our magenta-stained fingers have collected more than four kilograms of berries. Nibbling our warm-from-the-sun strawberries, we stop at another farm to buy lettuce, cabbage and kale. Our baskets brimming with food, we return to the city to feast.

Pros and Cons

+ Supporting local producers
- Berry-stained fingers
- Fishy daypack

RESEARCH FOOD SOURCES
CAERPHILLY AND YOU'LL FIND
GRATE LOCAL PRODUCE

Food Wizardry

Food technologists devote their lives to transforming raw ingredients into supermarket-worthy produce. Take transglutaminase: this enzyme enables meat processors to bind together multiple pieces of meat, knitting small fragments into a satisfyingly large steak. Its protein-binding powers are also useful in making fish sticks and meatballs. Beavers make a surprise contribution to many ice creams. Mammal-derived castoreum usually masquerades as 'natural flavouring' on ingredients labels. There's something fishy about your beer, too: isinglass, extracted from swim bladders, is often used in 'finings', added to beer to accelerate the process of separating sediment from the finished product. Fortunately no flavour is imparted during the process.

ADVENTURE #8

Memory Lane

LET YOUR INNER CHILD RUN WILD. INDULGE EVERY WHIM AS YOU TRIP THROUGH THE HAPPIEST LOCATIONS OF YOUR CHILDHOOD.

What you'll need

HAPPY MEMORIES
ACCESS TO CHILDHOOD HAUNTS

Instructions

YOUR INNER CHILD WANTS TO PERFORM CARTWHEELS IN THE PARK, EAT COOKIES FOR BREAKFAST, AND CHASE PIGEONS THROUGH THE MAIN SQUARE.

THINK ABOUT WHERE YOU WERE HAPPIEST AS A CHILD - A PARK YOU USED TO PLAY IN, A DUCK POND WHERE YOU SCATTERED BREAD - AND TAKE A TRIP DOWN MEMORY LANE. DON'T HOLD BACK: IF YOU LOVED KICKING A BALL OR CHASING SQUIRRELS, ABANDON SELF-CONSCIOUSNESS AND UNLEASH YOUR INNER CHILD.

IF CHILDHOOD HAUNTS AREN'T CLOSE TO HOME, RECREATE A LONG-ABANDONED PASTIME. NEWSPAPER-WRAPPED CHIPS BY THE BEACH, HOSE-PIPE WARS IN YOUR GARDEN, EATING CAKE ICING-FIRST...IF IT MAKES YOU SQUEAL WITH GLEE, DO IT.

COMPLEXITY ★ ☆ ☆ ☆ ☆

39

Case study
Ali Lemer, Native New Yorker

My hometown has changed in countless ways since I ran around it in pigtails; could I recreate my childhood New York? First I visit William Greenberg Desserts for my once-favourite treat: their signature rich, moist brownies. For good measure, I also get a Black & White Cookie (another NYC speciality), which I polish off walking to the pocket-sized Central Park Zoo.

It's a hot, sweaty day, so I duck into the penguin building; the cool air smells like old fish but I'm transported with delight by these endearing creatures. Though I'm conflicted about wild animals in captivity, I'm still grateful for the chance to see them.

I devour my brownie on the bus to the American Museum of Natural History. I recall seeing the same fusty dioramas of taxidermied animals years ago. Best is the Hall of Ocean Life, with its gigantic blue whale floating above our heads. After a 2003 refurbishment it looks better and more colourful than before. It's comforting to know that this quintessential icon from my past will be there for future generations.

I buy my inner child a chocolate ice cream and walk across Central Park to the Ancient Playground (an apt description for how I feel being there). It's just as I remember: a huge brick pyramid with ladders, ramparts, tunnels and slides. I clamber up awkwardly and whoosh down smoothly, barely suppressing a whee! Then again. And again. Who cares about adult responsibilities? I think I'll get another dessert.

Pros and Cons

+ Penguins!
- Cavities

Medicinal Memories

Nostalgia is as soothing as a warm bath, but it also has power. Recalling fond memories has a measurable positive effect on mental health, making 'reminiscence therapy' an increasingly common treatment for patients suffering with dementia or depression. Taking its cue from reminiscence therapy, an enterprising Australian radio station, Silver Memories, hired retired broadcasters to DJ music from the 1940s in retirement homes. Going a step further, the 'Memory Lane' village near Bristol in the UK faithfully mimics a 1950s-style post office, greengrocers and pub, even decking the walls with old Oxo adverts, to immerse elderly patients in the sights and smells of their childhood.

NATURAL HISTORY MUSEUMS: INSPIRING THE NEXT GENERATION OF PARK RANGERS (AND BEAR TAXIDERMISTS)

41

Water Cure

INDULGE IN A SPA DAY ON A TINY BUDGET,
WITH THE BONUS OF SNOOPING THE MOST
PRIVATE ROOM OF A FRIEND'S HOUSE.

What you'll need

FLUFFY TOWELS

BATH BOMB, BATH SALTS OR OTHER UNGUENTS

AN UNWITTING FRIEND'S BATHROOM

Instructions

SOAKING IN TOASTY WARM WATER BENEFITS BODY AND SOUL, BUT TRAGICALLY YOU DON'T LIVE DOWN THE ROAD FROM ICELAND'S BLUE LAGOON. WORSE STILL, YOUR OWN BATHROOM IS IN A SORRY STATE WITH A TANGLE OF HAIR AROUND THE PLUGHOLE AND AN ONGOING COLD WAR ABOUT NEVER CHANGING THE LOO ROLL.

THE SOLUTION IS A DIY SPA DAY: TEMPORARY ESCAPISM TO THE BATHROOM OF A FRIEND OR RELATIVE FOR A CHANGE OF SCENE (AND A DISCREET SNOOP). IDENTIFY A FRIEND WITH A FANCY BATHROOM, SEIZE A LOAD OF BATH PRODUCTS YOU NEVER GET AROUND TO USING, SLIDE INTO SILKY WATERS, AND SIGH AHHHH...

COMPLEXITY ★ ✫ ✫ ✫

43

Case study
Michael Clerizo, Clandestine Curist

'We've got the builders in and they're painting the ceiling in the bathroom,' I say to my friend William, fibbing madly. 'Can I use yours?' William, from Hong Kong, is one of my closest friends. We leap into his people-mover and drive round to his house.

On the way I ask if his shower has any idiosyncrasies. Does the shower curtain go inside or outside the tub? Also, I don't trust my footing on unfamiliar, wet surfaces. Does he have a shower mat? Other people's bathrooms are quirky and sometimes treacherous places, and I like to be prepared.

Arriving at William's I discover that the bathroom is a bright-yellow and blue room. Eleven orange ceramic frogs are arranged around one corner of the bathtub. Eleven white candles are arranged at the head of the tub. A shelf is full of bottles and jars. I'm curious to know what's inside these exotic vessels but all the labels are in Chinese. I open each one, peer inside and inhale, hoping to recognise a scent. I can identify the contents of only two: one jar has a creamy liquid with a jasmine aroma; the other is a blue bottle containing bath salts.

After turning on the taps and tipping in the bath salts I add a few drops of the jasmine cream. As the tub fills with water, the room fills with fragrance. Using some matches I find in the cabinet over the sink, I light the candles on the corner of the tub. Luxuriating in the hot, scented water, I shave, lie back and relax. I glance up at the still unknown bottles on the shelf and consider learning Chinese...

Pros and Cons

+ Escapism
− Learning how poorly your bathroom compares

Stranger Spas

Birch-branch floggings in Russia and ice-cold plunge pools in Finland may sound masochistic, but the most intriguing wellness therapies endure in Japan. Nightingale droppings are an ingredient in some Japanese face-creams, a throwback to the centuries-old practice of geisha using precious bird poop to preserve youthful skin. On a grander scale, Hakone's Yunessun Spa offers guests the chance to splash around in green tea, coffee, *sake* or red wine-infused water, all believed to be tonics for the skin. The quest for tight pores finds even stranger expression in Tokyo, where the Clinical-Salon Ci:z.Labo offers mollusc massage. Spa-goers submit to snails slithering on their faces to benefit from the slime's hyaluronic acid, protein and antioxidants. What a treat.

THE BLUE LAGOON IN REYKJAVIK, ICELAND: FOR BATHERS WHO PREFER SULPHUROUS STEAM TO FRAGRANT BATH SALTS

45

Searching the Subconscious

FREE YOUR SUBCONSCIOUS MIND TO LEAD THE WAY, AND ANALYSE YOUR SECRET URGES...

What you'll need

AN ID TO UNLEASH

A SUPEREGO TO REEL YOU BACK

Instructions

CHOOSE A LOCATION THAT'S FAMILIAR BUT NOT STRONGLY ASSOCIATED WITH ANY PARTICULAR ROUTINE (YOUR COMMUTE OR SHOPPING STREET ARE OUT). PERHAPS A PARK YOU'VE PASSED THROUGH BRIEFLY, OR A RESIDENTIAL NEIGHBOURHOOD THAT YOU'VE ENCOUNTERED BUT NEVER SPENT MUCH TIME IN.

CREATE A WALKING STREAM OF CONSCIOUSNESS BY STROLLING, STOPPING OR SKIPPING WHEREVER YOUR WHIMS DICTATE. IF YOUR FIRST THOUGHT IS TO SIT ON THE GRASS, RESIST YOUR SUPEREGO CHASTISING THAT YOUR JEANS MIGHT GET MUDDY; IT'S A SMALL PRICE TO PAY FOR SUBLIMINAL DISCOVERY.

COMPLEXITY ✷ ✷ ✷ ✷ ✷

47

Case study
Kachael Antony, Self-Aware Stroller

It's not easy to unleash one's subconscious in the hostile environs of middle-class suburbia. I half expected it to launch vicious attacks onto passers-by, or reveal a deeply depraved sexual perversity, but alas there was no such response. Nonetheless I found myself strolling along aimlessly. I will recount what followed as if it were a dream (psychoanalytic interpretations appear in brackets)...

To my right is a graveyard behind a seemingly endless steel post fence (= life journey). I see a house for sale that's open for inspection. I enter (= desire to return to the womb), and see a white coat hanging in the hallway (= a wedding dress) and a large print of yellow roses over an empty white bed (= thwarted fertility). The house is not to my liking (= fear of commitment), so I continue to the graveyard (= morbid tendencies).

I arrive at an empty grave without a name (= my own mortality), where I find a broken ceramic wreath of roses (= loss of childhood innocence). I place a circular portion of the wreath at the grave of poor old Thomas Keneally, long dead from Ireland (= make peace with my ancestral past). I retrace my steps (= look inwards) to reach the commemorative Elvis grave (= father figure), whom I find strangely attractive (= Oedipus complex), and see an 'Exit' sign (= solution). I take my blue suede shoes in that direction and make my way back to my car (= embrace life once again).

Back at the car I give a mental wink to my subconscious. 'So,' I say. 'Who's driving?'

Pros and Cons
+ Heightened self-awareness
- Uncomfortable truths

FOR DEEPER SELF-
KNOWLEDGE, OBEY YOUR
SUPPRESSED URGES (BUT
NOT THE ONES THAT'LL
GET YOU ARRESTED)

Channelling The Surreal

Sigmund Freud, the founder of psychoanalysis, theorised that individual personalities were formed in part by the interplay between the id, the ego and the superego. His ideas were tremendously influential, not just in the behavioural sciences but in the arts. The Surrealists employed various tactics to access the unconscious, including automatic drawing and writing, attempting to see the waking world through the dual vision of the conscious and the subconscious minds. André Breton's first 'automatic' sentence was: 'There is a man cut in two by the window', which came to him as he was falling asleep one night. He later described it as being like 'a knock on the windowpane of consciousness'.

49

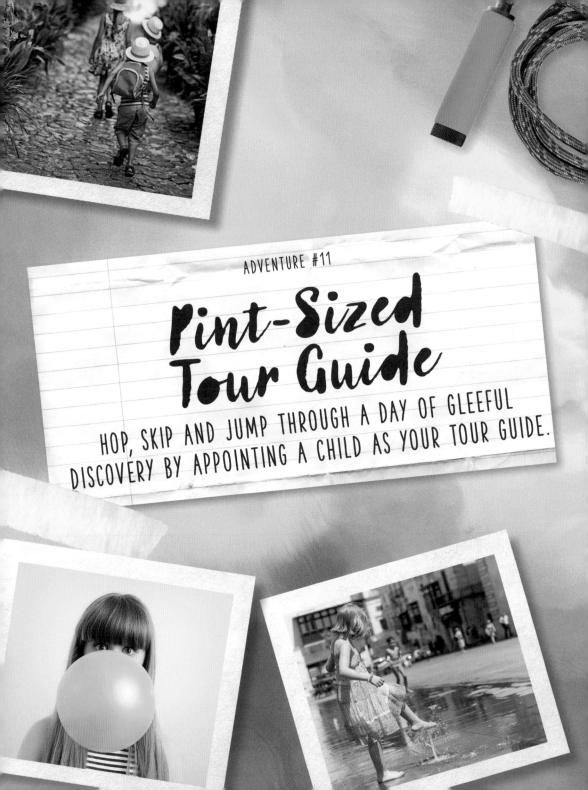

Pint-Sized Tour Guide

HOP, SKIP AND JUMP THROUGH A DAY OF GLEEFUL DISCOVERY BY APPOINTING A CHILD AS YOUR TOUR GUIDE.

What you'll need

A CHILD AGED SIX OR OVER

A MODE OF TRANSPORT

TOTAL LACK OF SELF-CONSCIOUSNESS

Instructions

NOMINATE A CHILD AS YOUR TOUR GUIDE FOR THE DAY. YOUR PINT-SIZED GUIDE CAN BE YOUR OWN CHILD OR A FRIEND'S, PROVIDED THEIR PARENTS CAN COPE WITHOUT THEIR BOSSINESS FOR A DAY (THEY CAN THANK YOU LATER).

MAKE IT CLEAR THAT USUAL RULES OF SAFETY APPLY, BUT OTHERWISE THE CHILD IS IN CHARGE OF DECIDING ON A FUN DAY OUT (AS LONG AS IT'S LOCAL). WE'D ADVISE AGAINST HAVING A PAIR OR A GROUP OF CHILDREN TAKE THE REINS, UNLESS YOU WANT THE ADVENTURE TO DESCEND INTO MAYHEM.

COMPLEXITY ★★☆☆☆

Case study
Daniel McCrohan,
Guildford-based Travel Dad

'Get up, dad! I'm tour guide for the day!' screams my seven-year-old daughter Yoyo. Being a travel writer is a dream job for me, but even I'm not this excited going to work.

Over breakfast she briefs me on the plan: den-making on the Downs (sounds cool); cycling in Stoke Park (fine by me); skipping around Guildford Castle (hang on, did she just say skipping?). Tentatively, I give her a thumbs-up and follow her to the castle.

Guildford's 900-year-old Norman fort is one of my favourite spots in town, but apparently it isn't fun enough for a seven-year-old, so Yoyo's brought her skipping rope to jazz things up. She can even skip while running (how do they do that?). 'Your turn, dad.' She passes me the rope. I fail, miserably.

It's mercilessly hot, so without a second thought Yoyo adds swimming to the agenda. We cycle to Stoke Park, which happens to have a large, free-to-use outdoor paddling pool. It's packed, of course, and despite my remonstrations she drags me in.

Cooler and calmer, we head up to the North Downs, a ridge of chalk hills that runs from Surrey to the White Cliffs of Dover. Yoyo's heard there's a den up here and we soon find it, start building our own, and find time for a spot of woodcraft. Yoyo makes a stick sword... which I have to carry home, because she's skipping all the way.

'Best day ever, dad,' she says. 'Can we do whatever I say tomorrow, too?'

Pros and Cons

+ Nurturing young leadership potential
- Realising your knees aren't what they were

CEDE CONTROL TO A
KID AND YOU'LL TASTE
SNOWFLAKES, CUPCAKES
AND POSSIBLY CRAYONS

Miniature Monarchs

If your child has a knack for giving orders, they'll be delighted to learn about the grand tradition of baby monarchs. One such slobbering sovereign was King John I of France, crowned on the same day he was born. Incredibly, King John isn't technically the youngest monarch to be crowned. Persian king Shah Shapur II was declared king while still in the womb, with a crown placed on his mother's belly. A regency ruled the empire until his teens, after which he scored numerous successes during his 70-year reign, conquering Roman provinces and championing Zoroastrianism at the cost of horrific persecution of Christians...childhood milestones will never seem the same again.

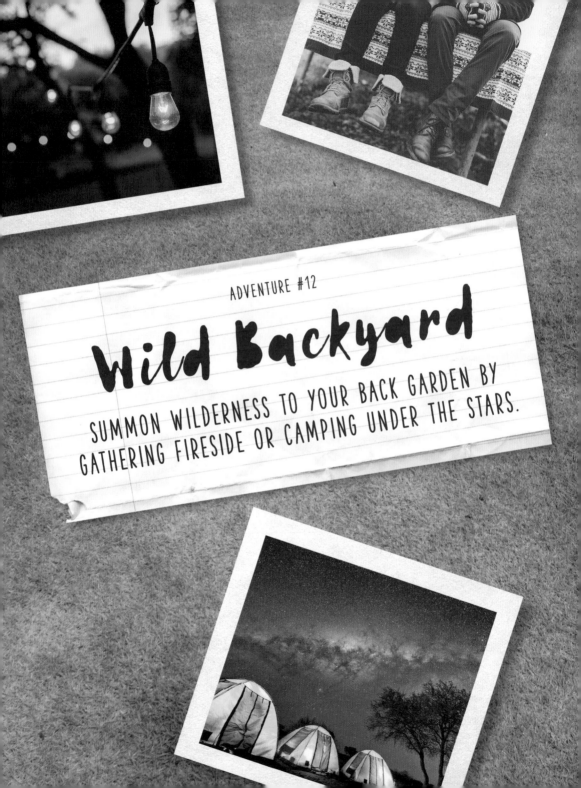

ADVENTURE #12

Wild Backyard

SUMMON WILDERNESS TO YOUR BACK GARDEN BY GATHERING FIRESIDE OR CAMPING UNDER THE STARS.

What you'll need

FIREPIT AND FIRELIGHTERS

SLEEPING BAG AND/OR TENT

MARSHMALLOWS

Instructions

RECREATE THE COMMUNITY VIBE OF A CAMPING TRIP IN YOUR BACKYARD, WITH THE HELP OF A FIREPIT. ACQUIRE A PORTABLE ONE IF CONSTRUCTING A BRICK-LINED KILN FEELS LIKE OVERKILL. GATHER FRIENDS, ARM THEM WITH MARSHMALLOWS, CRACK OPEN SOME BEERS. WHO KNOWS A GOOD GHOST STORY?

FOR A MORE SEDATE EXPERIENCE, SET UP A TENT IN YOUR GARDEN AND SNUGGLE INTO A SLEEPING BAG, DELIGHTING IN THE KNOWLEDGE THAT A PROPER BATHROOM IS WONDERFULLY CLOSE BY...

COMPLEXITY ★ ★ ★ ★ ★

57

Case study
Kerry Christiani, Firepit Fan

How easy it is to overlook the charm of our backyards. Many moons ago, I would only venture into the garden on summer days. The idea of clammy waterproofs and struggling to barbecue sausages under a leaking umbrella filled me with a very British sense of dread. As for sitting outside on a damp winter's night – why would you? Perhaps because with a few simple additions, a backyard can become a little corner of wilderness where we can unplug from the mundanities of urban life and tune into nature – no matter where we live, no matter what the time of year.

Central to the wilderness-in-the-backyard concept for me is the firepit. Brick-built ones are the dream, but I love my little portable one, fashioned from an old washing machine drum. It's a thing of beauty. Toss on a few logs and I can dream away, staring into the hypnotic flickering flames. Invite some friends and I can cook over it: crumpets on forks, marshmallows, dampers. It's like being a kid all over again. Light garden torches or lanterns, get out the tartan picnic blankets, crack open some beers or wine and the holiday atmosphere is complete. Singing, guitar strumming, impromptu jam sessions, alfresco Twister – anything goes at a firepit party.

As the night creeps in, so the atmosphere in the garden changes. This is the hour now when the embers of the fire are glowing and the mood has switched to one of quiet contemplation. Nocturnal birds warble in silhouetted trees, foxes skulk in the shadows, a tentative moon hovers in the night sky. Someone starts to talk about star constellations, picking out the Big Dipper and the Plough in the near-total darkness, and for an instant it feels almost wild.

Pros and Cons

+ Communing with nature
+ Frolics with friends
- Chance of rain
- Smoky clothes

THERE'S AN ANNUAL
MARSHMALLOW TOASTING DAY
ON 30 AUGUST, BUT WE WON'T
HOLD YOU TO THAT DATE

Fiery Beginnings

The ability to create and control fire was a turning point for early humans, not only so we could cook food and keep warm. Fires were pivotal for early human culture, acting as focal points for social gatherings. Humans who weren't able to build fires themselves were drawn by their warmth and emboldened to form small communities with those who could. With early humans spending so much time huddled together by fires, it's theorised that the need to develop more complex languages arose. Additionally, the light source provided by fire allowed human activity to continue after sunset, increasing the opportunity for early forms of art. Even for *Homo erectus*, then, there's something irresistibly romantic about the glow of a fire...

TOAST MORE THAN
MARSHMALLOWS: WE
SUGGEST HALLOUMI,
STRAWBERRIES, AND
LETTERS FROM YOUR EX

59

Social Media Slave

DO YOU TRUST YOUR SOCIAL MEDIA FOLLOWERS? BE LED ASTRAY FOR A DAY BY OBEYING THEIR EVERY COMMAND.

What you'll need

ACTIVE SOCIAL MEDIA FOLLOWERS

Instructions

1. ANNOUNCE ON YOUR MOST FREQUENTLY USED SOCIAL NETWORK THAT YOU'RE PLANNING TO SPEND A DAY OBEYING INSTRUCTIONS SENT BY YOUR FOLLOWERS.

2. BE SPECIFIC ON THE TIME AND DATE OF YOUR SOCIAL MEDIA EXPERIMENT, GIVING YOUR FOLLOWERS A FEW DAYS' NOTICE.

3. MENTION YOUR APPROXIMATE (NOT EXACT) LOCATION, SO THEY CAN SEND SUITABLE SUGGESTIONS. URGE THEM TO KEEP IT CLEAN (FAILING THAT, REMEMBER YOU HAVE A 'BLOCK' BUTTON).

4. WHEN THE DAY COMES, PROMPT YOUR FOLLOWERS FOR DIRECTIONS, ACTIVITIES AND CHALLENGES, AND SEE WHERE THE HIVE MIND LEADS YOU.

COMPLEXITY ★ ★ ★ ★ ☆

Case study
Belinda Dixon, Digital Adventurer

I'm heading out, but I have no idea where. Today I'm exploring London through disjointed instructions received via social media. The first command is: 'Jump aboard a bus, get off after the fourth stop.' I'm now in unfamiliar territory.

'Follow someone with a bag for 100 paces (subtly so you don't get arrested),' comes the next order. I follow my mark; very James Bond.

'Walk north until you see someone with red hair, then turn east until you see grass, and south until you see something pink,' insists a new message. I resist the urge to ignore the instruction to go north (it's a gritty neighbourhood). A red-haired woman sends me east, to a shabby apartment block. A patch of grass diverts me through a squeaky gate. The sounds of a Latin dance class filter from an old building – alive to my surroundings, I realise that'd be fun to try. Pink flowers prompt me to ask: what next?

'Flip a coin: heads go left, tails go right.' It's heads, towards town. I'm not lost, but I'm not entirely sure where I am. 'Assign an action to each of the six sides of a die; roll and walk,' my phone pings. I roll a one (go left) then a two (go right), then a three (go in) – now I'm inside a Portuguese bakery I've never noticed before.

I roll a five (ask a question): 'How much is a *pastel de nata*?' A bargain at £1.

'Go down to the Barbican,' comes the command. Easily done. 'Now find a cocktail to match the letters of your name.' Sipping a Blue Lagoon, I ponder re-discovering a city that became strange to me. I'll do it again.

Pros and Cons

+ Zany suggestions
- Creepy direct messages

COCKTAILS, CUSTARD TARTS...
IT'S RARE FOR THE INTERNET TO
SUGGEST A SWIFT JOG AND A
PROTEIN SHAKE

Hold My Beer...

Like a gaggle of slightly drunk friends, social networks can act like an echo chamber for daft ideas. In the earlier days of the internet, the craze was planking: lying horizontal in increasingly bizarre locations, and sharing a planking pic on social media to impress the world. Online trends got messier with public milkings, cats lodged into slices of bread, and 'baguetting' (not as rude as it sounds).

But these are child's play compared with 'extreme selfies', where photogenic Instagram users dangle from high-rise buildings in the name of online stardom. Russian daredevil Angela Nikolau has proved herself queen of this risky meme, posting self-portraits where she sunbathes on skyscraper ledges and balances on scaffolding. We miss the internet's innocent old days.

63

Life Swap

ABANDON YOUR HABITS, HOBBIES, MORNING LIE-IN (AND MAYBE YOUR DIGNITY): FOR ONE DAY ONLY, YOU'RE SWITCHING LIVES WITH A FRIEND.

What you'll need

A FRIEND TO SWAP LIVES WITH

AN OVERNIGHT BAG

Instructions

1. CHOOSE A PERSON TO SWAP LIVES WITH FOR A DAY. THEY COULD BE A FRIEND, FAMILY MEMBER, OR A CASUAL ACQUAINTANCE WHO'S EAGER TO EVANGELISE THEIR SUPERIOR ROUTINE. YOUR IDEAL LIFE SWAP PARTNER LIVES IN A DIFFERENT NEIGHBOURHOOD AND HAS CONTRASTING HOBBIES TO YOUR OWN.

2. CRASH AT THEIR HOUSE THE NIGHT BEFORE THE EXPERIMENT BEGINS, SO YOU CAN EXPERIENCE THEIR ROUTINE FROM MORNING UNTIL NIGHT.

3. EMBRACE THEIR HABITS AS FULLY AS YOU CAN, WHETHER THEY INVOLVE 6AM YOGA, SLEEPING UNTIL NOON, OR A PALEO SUGAR-FREE DIET. NO WHINGING.

4. NOW 'REWARD' YOUR BUDDY WITH THE CHANCE TO TRY YOUR ROUTINE...

COMPLEXITY ★ ★ ★ ★ ☆

65

Case study
Louise Bastock, Lazy Weekender

As someone who values sleep above anything at the weekends, being shaken awake at 8.30am by my sister, eager to get to her local bakery before the crowds, was a shock. But it's true, the early bird does catch the best croissants. Loaded up with goodies I follow her to Hampstead Heath for a stroll, stumbling upon a quaint farmers' market and soaking up a side of the park I've never explored before, all because we approached it from her neighbourhood.

Surely it's time for a nap – but apparently our day is just beginning. We slurp smoothies at a local cafe – it's full of 'regulars' who are chatting to one another, and even chatting to me (am I still in London?) – before getting manicures at the salon across the road. I rarely get beauty treatments so this feels highly indulgent.

We wander down the backstreets on the way to pick up some groceries at her local organic food store. The sounds of the city die down and I'm treated to streets that feel like country lanes, their houses painted an array of cheerful colours. Living in a busy city I'm always concerned about getting from A to B as quickly as possible, so I never think to detour into smaller residential areas. As we walk, my sister points out all the details I would usually overlook – intricate designs on people's front doors, beautiful plants spilling from front gardens, chalk drawings on the pavement from local kids.

We close the day with a cheeky ice cream in my sister's garden. I listen to the unfamiliar sounds of her neighbourhood winding down. Surrounded by thick, heavy greenery, the city beyond feels a world away.

Pros and Cons

+ Free tour guide
+ No decision fatigue
- Other people's lives are expensive

PASTRIES AREN'T A MANDATORY FEATURE OF A LIFE SWAP, BUT THEY CERTAINLY DON'T HURT

Plagiarised Personalities

Walking a mile in someone else's shoes has long been considered morally instructive; the same can't be said for concocting a new identity. Tell that to George Psalmanazar, one of the world's most famous imposters. Psalmanazar toured Great Britain in the 18th century, lecturing about his 'native' Formosa (Taiwan). The only snag? He'd never set foot there. A career forger, Psalmanazar started by impersonating an Irish pilgrim, then adopting a Japanese persona (both ruses were rumbled). But Formosa was almost unknown – enabling Psalmanazar to invent a polygamous, cannibalistic society where gold genital plates were the height of fashion and snake blood was a popular breakfast food.

FRESH AIR, EDIFYING VIEWS...BUT FEAR NOT, YOU CAN RESUME YOUR UNHEALTHY ROUTINE AT THE END OF THE EXPERIMENT

Make-Believe Backpacking

EMBRACE THE BACKPACKER LIFESTYLE WITHOUT LEAVING TOWN – NO BONE-RATTLING BUS JOURNEYS OR EXOTIC ILLNESSES REQUIRED.

What you'll need

A TRAVEL GUIDEBOOK ABOUT YOUR AREA

YOUR BEST BACKPACKER OUTFIT (TOURIST T-SHIRT, BEADED NECKLACE...)

Instructions

1. PACK A RUCKSACK WITH EVERYTHING A BACKPACKER COULD NEED: CAMERA, SUNBLOCK, SPORK, FLIP-FLOPS AND - CRUCIALLY - A GUIDEBOOK.

2. GET A RIDE TO THE CLOSEST AIRPORT. ONCE YOU ARRIVE, CAST OFF THE SHACKLES OF YOUR LIFE AS A LOCAL. NOW IS THE MOMENT TO ASSUME YOUR NEW GUISE, A BACKPACKER NEW IN TOWN.

3. CATCH THE CHEAPEST TRANSPORT FROM THE AIRPORT BACK TO TOWN AND HAUL YOUR RUCKSACK TO THE NEAREST HOSTEL RECOMMENDED IN YOUR BOOK.

4. ENJOY A DAY OF SHOESTRING SIGHTSEEING BEFORE RETIRING TO PARTY HARD WITH FELLOW HOSTEL GUESTS (OR BE LULLED BY THEIR CHORUS OF SNORES).

COMPLEXITY ✱ ✱ ✱ ✱ ✱

69

Case study
Alex Landrigan, Writer & Bluffing Backpacker

I set off from Melbourne airport, bound for a hostel in St Kilda. My travels must be limited to my guidebook – which, ironically enough, I have in part authored. I am not quite local, not quite stranger. I am either a local stranger or a strange local.

Once I've alighted from the bus downtown I head instinctively to the Victoria Market for some lunch. I know a stall that sells the most delicious pizzas and good, strong, aromatic coffee; fortunately, it's listed in my guide.

My hostel is described as 'friendly'. The reception notice board is covered with ads for job vacancies, including one offering $150 for 'nude photographic work'.

I decide to go sightseeing. At Federation Square's art gallery, I jump the queue to a blockbuster exhibition by telling the staff I've left my gloves inside. As a backpacker one spends hours queuing, but as the world's only time-poor backpacker I simply can't wait.

Back at my lodgings, a bunch of young Brits sip their tepid beers and watch the telly. They must be wondering what brought them here to spend a northern summer in the southern cold, watching a code of football as obscure as it is incomprehensible.

After the football game, I retire to my quarters. The bunk bed sways to my slightest movement while, downstairs at an English-themed pub, the crowd sings along to a covers band – 'Those were the best days of my life'.

Pros and Cons

+ Thrilling anonymity
- Creaking bunk beds

JUST FOR A WEEKEND,
BE ONE OF THOSE
TOURISTS YOU LOVE
COMPLAINING ABOUT

ST KILDA BEAC

Trail-Blazing Backpacker

Long before the first travel selfie was posted, even before hippies dawdled across Asia in the 1950s, Giovanni Francesco Gemelli Careri blazed the trail for backpackers. Travel for pleasure wasn't unknown in the late 17th century, but it was a pastime of the rich, usually in the form of a lavish 'Grand Tour'. Winging it on a budget was unheard of, but Gemelli Careri spent years travelling the world. The thrifty Italian bought spices, cloth and dried fruit along the way, selling them for a small profit whenever he reached a new location. He compiled his tales from the road into *Giro del Mondo* – but at six volumes long, we'd suggest travelling with a much lighter Lonely Planet guide instead.

11

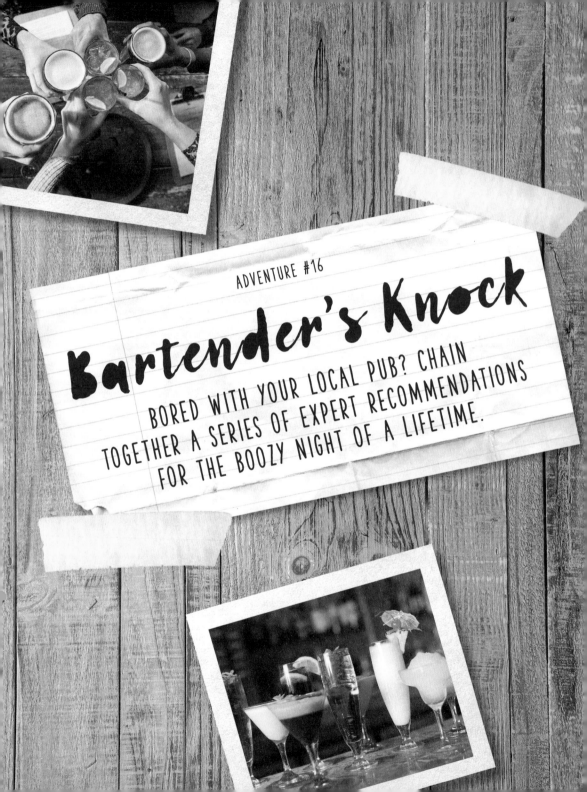

ADVENTURE #16

Bartender's Knock

BORED WITH YOUR LOCAL PUB? CHAIN TOGETHER A SERIES OF EXPERT RECOMMENDATIONS FOR THE BOOZY NIGHT OF A LIFETIME.

What you'll need

WILLING ACCOMPLICES

DUTCH COURAGE

Instructions

WORD TO THE WISE: DON'T PLAY BARTENDER'S KNOCK ON AN EMPTY STOMACH...

1. BEGIN IN A LOCAL PUB, WHERE YOU AND YOUR FELLOW PLAYERS WILL ORDER YOUR FAVOURITE DRINKS.

2. STRIKE UP A CONVERSATION WITH A BARTENDER TO FIND OUT THEIR SIGNATURE DRINK AND THEIR PREFERRED LOCAL PLACE TO DRINK IT.

3. PROCEED TO THEIR SUGGESTED BOOZER AND ORDER THE RECOMMENDED DRINK, REPEATING THE EXERCISE WITH BAR STAFF THERE.

4. REPEAT UNTIL YOUR THIRST IS SATED, AND CERTAINLY STOP WHILE YOU STILL HAVE THE CAPACITY TO COMMUNICATE YOUR HOME ADDRESS TO A CABBIE.

COMPLEXITY ✱ ✱ ✱ ✱ ✱

Case study
Tom Parkinson,
Clapham Pub-Crawler

We start our experiment in our front room in Clapham, London, drinking super-strength Belgian beer. As there is no barman, Jen, my obliging housemate, nominates her current hotspot, Dixies, and for the next round a cheap bottle of Foster's.

We are served by Jonny, possibly Spanish, who directs us (rather unimaginatively) to the Fine Line chain pub. Then, on the advice of our bargirl Bea, we dash across the road to SO.UK, über-fashionable and slightly Arabic-themed, for tequila shots.

Next we are dispatched to Revolution, with orders to try an old-fashioned. This causes our first setback of the evening: Revolution doesn't do old-fashioneds. We order bourbon instead, confusing poor barman Peter so much that he forgets to charge us. He does, however, direct us to the Falcon, a good old-fashioned (sorry) pub which, in time-honoured British style, closes just as we get there.

It's late and the Falcon staff's suggestion of a nightclub doesn't appeal. Taking creative licence, we head for the nearest open bar, the Bierodrome, for Belgian fruit beer. By now we've had enough – bus, pizza and bed takes us to the end of our journey.

We come home with several new friends, a whole clutch of bar recommendations, a dozen photos of confused bar staff and, for some reason, rude words written in marker pen on our knuckles. What more could you want from a night out?

Pros and Cons

+ Expert advice

– The morning after

IF YOU SEE THREE PUMPS, PLAY
ON...IF YOU SEE SIX, TIME TO
ALE A CAB HOME

Hangover Tour

Bartender's Knock has painful,
if predictable, consequences: a
dry mouth, pounding temples and
existential dread. Before staggering to a
greasy spoon, why not take inspiration
from hangover cures around the
world? After getting pickled, drink
pickle juice – so goes the theory in
Poland and Russia. In Scandinavian
countries, revellers also reach their
trembling hands towards pickles,
they're usually atop *smørrebrød*, open-
faced rye-bread sandwiches. Hungover
Icelanders prefer a nourishing slice of
sviðasulta (head cheese), an aspic-set
sheep's-head pâté wobblier than your
sense of balance. It's no fried breakfast
but we'll take it over Scandinavia's
sauna cure for hangovers, a session of
intensive heat followed by a painful
plunge into ice-cold water.

EXPECT YOUR GAME OF
BARTENDER'S KNOCK TO
REACH A SWIFT END IF
YOU MEET BAR STAFF WITH
ENTHUSIASM FOR ABSINTHE

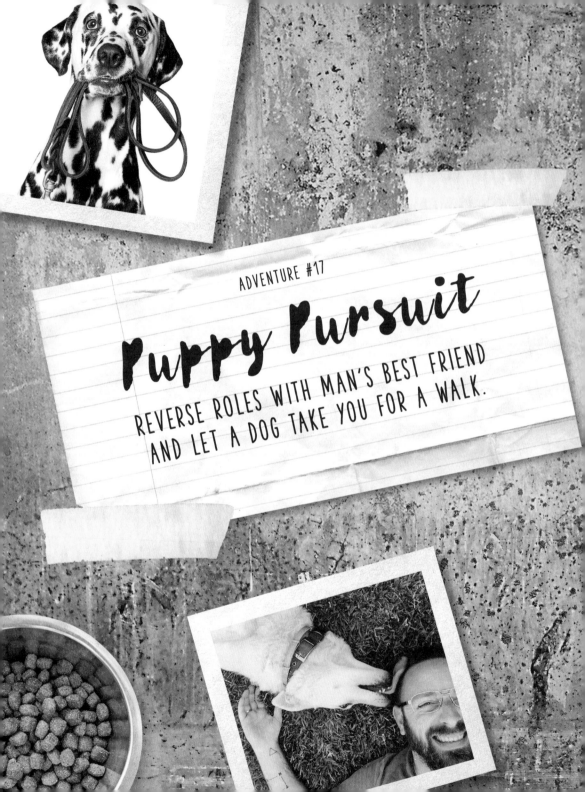

ADVENTURE #17

Puppy Pursuit

REVERSE ROLES WITH MAN'S BEST FRIEND AND LET A DOG TAKE YOU FOR A WALK.

What you'll need

AN INQUISITIVE CANINE

ALL-WEATHER SHOES

Instructions

WHAT HAPPENS WHEN A DOG TAKES THEIR HUMAN FOR A WALK, RATHER THAN THE OTHER WAY AROUND? PREPARE TO SCAMPER AFTER SQUIRRELS, INVESTIGATE UNKNOWN ODOURS AND MAKE NEW FRIENDS BY ALLOWING A FRIENDLY HOUND TO LEAD THE WAY.

YOU NEED TO BORROW A DOG FOR THIS ADVENTURE. DOGS TEND TO FOLLOW FAMILIAR PATHWAYS, SO BEING WALKED BY A FRIEND'S FOUR-LEGGED COMPANION WILL BE INFINITELY MORE INTERESTING THAN YOUR OWN.

COMPLEXITY ★ ☆ ☆ ☆ ☆

Case study
James Broad, Fateful Adventurer

It's another quiet evening in southern Montana, as my travelling pardner and I mosey down to the Two Goose Saloon for bison burgers and a coupla pints of Moose Drool. A snow-white malamute is pawing at the bar's glass front door.

The bartender invites the giddy dog inside. Soon enough we are introduced to Oscar, who curls up at our feet. After dinner, we follow Oscar outside for a walk around the one-horse town of Gardiner. Pausing at a coupla fire hydrants, we wander on to Oscar's home base – the Continental Divide White Water Company.

Oscar's surprised owners size me up and then ask if I am a kayaker. They explain that they are looking for a guinea pig to accompany a certain greenhorn guide down the river during her inaugural run. Would I care to join them?

As I shoehorn myself into my undersized fiberglass shell, Oscar gazes down from the bank with an anxious glint in his aquamarine eyes.

I flip over ass backwards in one of the first big rapids. In a breathless panic, I realise I have no idea how to wiggle my way out of the snug neoprene-spray skirt. When I surface, I see an enthusiastic canine scampering down the riverbank. 'He's come to save me,' I enthuse. But instead of heading for me, Oscar makes a beeline for the vintage wooden paddle that I ditched while submerged.

Back at the Two Goose that night, Oscar reappears through the swinging doors. We stick to our pints, lest we be bamboozled into another dawg-inspired adventure.

Pros and Cons

+ Chance meetings

– Near-death experiences

ADVENTURE #18

Fake Vacation

FEELING CHAINED TO THE 'BURBS OR LOCKED IN ROUTINE? REKINDLE URBAN THRILLS BY GOING INCOGNITO AT A LOCAL HOTEL.

What you'll need

HOTEL BOOKING

UNKNOWN NEIGHBOURHOOD

TRUSTED ACCOMPLICE

Instructions

THE EXCITEMENT OF BEING AN EXOTIC STRANGER NEEDN'T COST A PLANE TICKET. YOU JUST NEED STEALTH AND A HOTEL BOOKING FAR FROM YOUR USUAL HAUNTS.

FIRST, PICK AN OVERLOOKED PART OF YOUR TOWN: PERHAPS A HIP SUBURB YOU'VE NEVER SET FOOT IN. BOOK IN AT THE BEST HOTEL YOU CAN AFFORD, AND DRESS LIKE A CHIC OUT-OF-TOWNER: SUNGLASSES AND DANCING SHOES MANDATORY.

HEAVE YOUR SUITCASE INTO YOUR ROOM. SOAK UP SOME CONCIERGE SUGGESTIONS AND SECURE NIGHTLIFE TIPS FROM SOMEONE AT LEAST FIVE YEARS YOUNGER THAN YOU. MAKE NOTE OF THE LATEST HOUR YOUR HOTEL SERVES BREAKFAST, AND PARTY AS IF IT'S THE LAST DAY OF YOUR HOLIDAY.

COMPLEXITY ★ ★ ☆ ☆ ☆

Case study
James Bainbridge, Dad and Art Lover

Glass of Cape wine in hand, my wife waves me over. On one of the gallery's walls hangs a series of delicate pistols with petals clouding their transparent resin bodies.

To add some excitement to our suburban life of school runs and Lego castles, Leigh-Robin and I have checked into a hotel in the city centre. We have timed our one-night adventure to coincide with the monthly First Thursday, which enlivens the streets beneath Table Mountain with late-opening art galleries and pop-up bars.

We wander onto Bree Street, which has a vibey tapas bar for every good school in our sedate suburb, and find a vintage clothes market and a champagne bar. From the stallholders clad in faux fur and stonewash, to the glam cowgirl pouring bubbly, the bohemian characters of the inner city are exotic creatures to our parental eyes.

We drift on through the galleries, intoxicated by the feeling of being explorers in this arty community, with a hotel room to prove our outsider status. Warming to the role of curious travellers from a distant land, we enquire what lies beyond a VIP rope; our pioneering spirit is rewarded by a loft restaurant serving gourmet burgers. Later, I hear a fellow drinker say: 'I would've loved to live here in the 18th century: there were pirate ships in the bay and only about two houses on the slopes of Table Mountain.'

This romantic image reminds me that travellers have been visiting this city on the trade routes for centuries, that this spirit once persuaded me to call Cape Town home, and that we must return to this inner-city melting pot soon.

Pros and Cons

+ Contemporary art
+ Flight from routine
- Too much bubbly

COCKTAILS AT 4PM ON A
TUESDAY? TOTALLY COOL
ON A FAKE VACATION

ON A HOMETOWN HOLIDAY,
NO ONE NEED KNOW
YOUR TRUE AGE (OR HAIR
COLOUR)

Reality Check-In

A stay in a hotel involves a break from reality. Cleaners free you from domestic duties. No one scolds you for failing to make the bed. The thrilling alienation of hotels is a common cinematic theme. Director Sofia Coppola makes a Tokyo hotel the location for two jet-lagged foreign travellers struggling to find meaning in *Lost in Translation* (2003); and in *Somewhere* (2010), luxurious Chateau Marmont is the setting for celebrity ennui. Elsewhere, hotels become societies subject to their own rules. In *The Best Exotic Marigold Hotel* (2011), retirees draw strength from one another in the face of seismic life changes. Hotels encourage the redrawing of routine; tap into that feeling next time you sling a suitcase into your room.

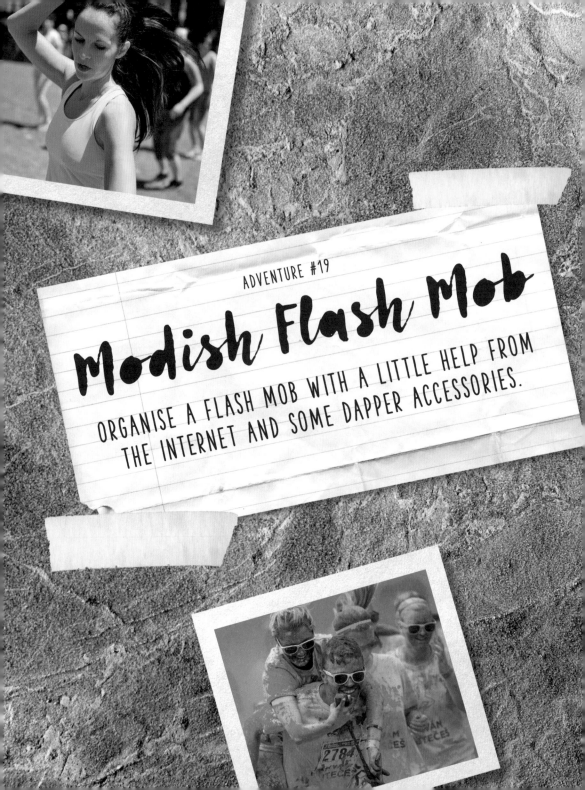

Modish Flash Mob

ORGANISE A FLASH MOB WITH A LITTLE HELP FROM THE INTERNET AND SOME DAPPER ACCESSORIES.

What you'll need

LUDICROUS CLOTHING (TIN-FOIL HATS, FEATHER BOAS...)
WELL-TRAFFICKED ONLINE FORUM

Instructions

YOUR MISSION: TO ASSEMBLE LIKE-MINDED IDLERS FOR A DRAMATIC BUT ULTIMATELY NONSENSICAL DEMONSTRATION.

1. DECIDE ON A THEME FOR YOUR IMPROMPTU GATHERING. MAKE IT LIGHT-HEARTED: SALSA DANCING IN TRAFALGAR SQUARE CLAD IN FEATHERS, WAVING GLOW-STICKS ALOFT IN CENTRAL STATION, YOUR IMAGINATION'S THE LIMIT.

2. PICK A TIME AND DATE, DECLARING YOUR INTENTION ON AN ONLINE FORUM SUCH AS GUMTREE OR YOUR LOCAL BRANCH OF REDDIT. STIFFEN YOUR RESOLVE AGAINST GUFFAWS FROM COMMENTERS, AND AWAIT EXPRESSIONS OF INTEREST.

3. ON THE DAY, GATHER MORE RECRUITS BY POSTING PICTURES ON SOCIAL MEDIA. IF THE CROWD SWELLS TOO BIG, SLIP AWAY AND DENY ALL KNOWLEDGE.

COMPLEXITY ★ ★ ★ ★ ★

Case study
Eric Hazard, Tinfoil-Capped New Yorker

'You look like the Tin Man,' cackles an old lady with a toothless grin. Admittedly, my appearance is comical: I have placed an aluminium deflector beanie on my head while I wait to meet my as-yet unidentified group of co-travellers.

Other than the toothless old woman, who apparently is above placing tinfoil on her own head, no-one even gives me a passing glance. Such is life in New York City.

For today's mission, strangers domed in tinfoil have agreed to rendezvous at City Hall. Once assembled, the group will proceed down Broadway to 'storm' the city's famous monument to capitalism: the Wall Street Bull.

In a city of eight million inhabitants, it's only me and two random women who have nothing better to do on a beautiful April day. We swap pleasantries and set off. Our saunter is a unifying experience, filled with exchanges of life stories.

After 15 minutes we have arrived at the core of capitalism's lie. One of the ladies proclaims that she will have her picture taken next and that we need volunteers! Once the multitude see how much fun the tinfoil-wearing whackos are having, others have no trouble posing with foil on their head for a photo.

Our multicultural final group includes a German expat who now calls the United States home, and a lost tourist whose next stop is to enquire about purchasing the Brooklyn Bridge. If there were any questions about our laboratory, I believe they have now been answered: New York is definitely the world's salad bowl.

Pros and Cons

+ New friends
− Cringe factor

CHOOSE AN ITEM OF CLOTHING
THAT ALL ATTENDEES OF YOUR
FLASH MOB CAN WEAR (PINK
SEQUINS SUIT EVERYONE)

Flesh Mob

Some surreal mass gatherings invoke a higher calling. Take Spencer Tunick: the very name of this conceptual artist can prompt huge crowds to drop their trousers. In Tunick's meticulously planned photoshoots, nude people become human sculptures. The sheer number of naked bodies involved in a Tunick shoot creates a fleshy landscape, stripping away any possibility of individuals feeling objectified. Hundreds of volunteers sign up for the opportunity to disrobe in locations including London's Cutty Sark, Dutch tulip fields and the Sydney Opera House. Tunick keeps unselfconscious art fans informed of forthcoming events, asking only that they register their skin tone so he can plan nude canvases down to the finest detail.

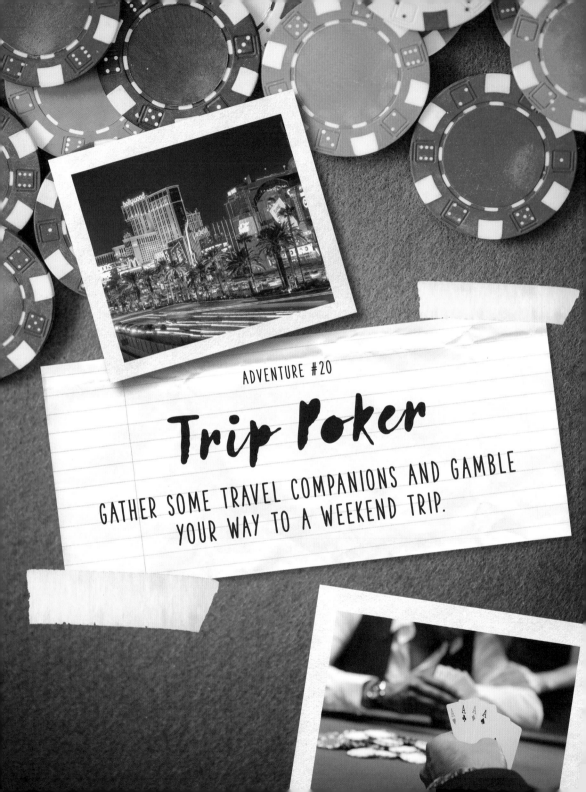

ADVENTURE #20

Trip Poker

GATHER SOME TRAVEL COMPANIONS AND GAMBLE
YOUR WAY TO A WEEKEND TRIP.

What you'll need

DICE OR A PACK OF CARDS

ONE OR MORE TRAVEL COMPANIONS

Instructions

IN TRIP POKER, PLAYERS PIT THEIR LUCK AGAINST ONE OTHER BY THROWING DICE OR DRAWING FROM A PACK OF CARDS. THE HIGHEST SCORER IN EACH ROUND WINS THE HONOUR OF DECIDING ON AN ESSENTIAL ELEMENT OF YOUR NEXT TRIP TOGETHER AS A GROUP. ROUND BY ROUND, THE WINNER DECIDES ON THE DESTINATION, MODE OF TRANSPORT, ACTIVITY, AND ACCOMMODATION.

BEFORE PLAYING, SET SOME RULES: YOU CAN VETO CERTAIN MODES OF TRANSPORT OR DESTINATIONS BEYOND A CERTAIN DISTANCE. ANNOUNCE AT THE BEGINNING OF EACH ROUND WHAT THE HIGHEST SCORER CAN DECIDE ABOUT THE TRIP.

REPEAT THE ROUNDS UNTIL YOU HAVE A HYBRID HOLIDAY COMBINING ALL THE WINNERS' SUGGESTIONS. THE REALLY FUN PART IS MAKING THE TRIP HAPPEN...

COMPLEXITY ★ ★ ★ ★ ★

Case study
Jöel Henry, Wager-Taking Wanderer

There are four of us around the table: our friends Robert and Christine, and Maïa and myself. There is green baize, subdued lighting and a bottle of very old whisky.

The game of trip poker is no laughing matter – the rounds may be very short but it's a dangerous game that can take you far and cost you dearly. Thanks to the modest roll of a four, I win the first round and with it the stake: the chance to choose the destination for our weekend break together. I choose Geneva, a city none of us has visited before.

Maïa wins the second round with a straight six, and the responsibility falls to her to choose the date for the weekend. Teetotaller Maïa attends drinking sessions under sufferance so the traitor takes advantage and chooses New Year's Eve for our trip.

Christine wins the third roll and chooses the type of accommodation. She decides without hesitation that we'll sleep in the car. (She's in charge of household finances.)

'We'll freeze to death,' complains Robert. 'We'll take blankets,' she replies firmly.

The last round is played in an atmosphere of extreme tension, until I roll the dice and my pitiful one puts an end to suspense. So the four of us will celebrate New Year's Eve in Geneva, sleeping in minus 15°C temperatures in a Mini Cooper – our only option, as Maïa and I (as ecological fundamentalists) have long forsaken car ownership. Despite its innocent exterior, Trip Poker is a cousin of Russian roulette.

Pros and Cons

+ Thrill of suspense
+ Team effort
- Sadistic friends

IT'S ALL FUN AND GAMES
UNTIL YOU GAMBLE YOUR WAY
TO A SWAMP-SIDE HOTEL IN
ALLIGATOR SEASON

Striking It Lucky

Ever wonder why some folk seem to have all the luck? Experimental psychologist Richard Wiseman concluded that there's an art to good fortune. Wiseman conducted studies on hundreds of volunteers, discovering that an individual's personality type is a good predictor of how 'lucky' they are. Upbeat personality types are more likely to notice opportunities and take a chance on new experiences (whether they involve dating, job opportunities or conversations with strangers).

This increases their chance of experiencing 'lucky' events. Pessimists and introverted personality types are likelier to second-guess opportunities or fail to notice them, reducing their chances of serendipitous outcomes. So in Trip Poker and in life, it's worth looking on the bright side.

WILL TRIP POKER LEAD
YOUR GROUP TO SNOOZE
IN A TOWNHOUSE OR
SQUABBLE IN A LEAKY
RIVERBOAT?

91

ADVENTURE #21

Local Summit

EVEN FAMILIAR SCENERY BECOMES MAGICAL WHEN SEEN FROM A BIRD'S-EYE VANTAGE POINT... SEEK A PEAK TO GAIN A DIZZYING NEW PERSPECTIVE.

What you'll need

LOCAL HIKING MAP

WALKING BOOTS & WEATHER-APPROPRIATE CLOTHING

Instructions

1. STUDY A LOCAL MAP TO SUSS OUT THE STEEPEST, HILLIEST AREAS NEAR YOU (SELECT 'TERRAIN' OR 'SATELLITE' ON ONLINE MAPS).

2. ONCE YOU'VE FOUND THE HIGHEST WALKABLE POINT NEAR YOU, PLAN A DAY-HIKE TO THE TOP, ARMED WITH MAPS, SNACKS, AND STURDY SHOES.

3. IF THE LAND'S FLATTER THAN A PANCAKE, WALK ANYWHERE YOU CAN FINISH WITH VERTIGINOUS VIEWS FROM A LIGHTHOUSE, SPIRE OR SKYSCRAPER.

4. TO TAKE RADIANT PHOTOS, AIM TO REACH THE SUMMIT IN LATE AFTERNOON. MAKE SURE YOU HAVE A SAFE PATH DOWN IF YOU'RE DESCENDING IN DARKNESS.

COMPLEXITY ★ ★ ☆ ☆ ☆

95

Case study
Patrick Kinsella,
Hyperopic Gravity Battler

I always experience an irresistible urge to head for the highest bit of whatever county, country or continent I'm exploring. This tendency has tested friendships and led to the cliff-edge of divorce. But my feet fidget until they're atop an apex point.

Strangely, though, I've ignored the tallest point near my house. One morning, the magnetism of the mount finally prevails and I cajole the brood to the base of our everyday Everest. Dorset's 191m Golden Cap is far from a mountain, but its blonde head is the loftiest point on Britain's south coast. It stares across the English Channel from Lyme Bay, a beautiful bitemark in the World Heritage-listed Jurassic Coast.

With the sun setting the sandstone summit ablaze, the family would rather explore the flat, fossil-strewn beaches below, but ice-cream themed bribes avert a mutiny. Ascending from the west, we pass St Gabriel's, an 800-year-old church, before following a serpentine trail tattooed on the torso of the hill by centuries of walkers.

The view robs us of any breath left after the steep climb, encompassing the entire 96-mile Jurassic Coast. Beneath our boots are dinosaur bones, bronze-age barrows, evidence of Viking invasions and the remains of beacons set to alert England to the approach of the Spanish Armada, Napoleon's navy and Hitler's bomb-laden Luftwaffe.

Even the kids are impressed. But they want their just desserts and I discern a siren's song emanating from the Anchor Inn, one-time hangout of smugglers who used Golden Cap as a lookout. Down we go, to toast a long-overlooked peak.

Pros and Cons

+ Killer views
- Post-pub exertions

Mind Over Mount

'Because it's there,' George Mallory famously replied when asked why he wanted to climb Mt Everest. Mallory embarked on the first British expeditions to Everest. He explained his urge to scale ever-greater heights as an aspect of humankind's will to conquer the universe. Everest is worlds away from summiting a hill, but the pace – which forces one's consciousness into the present moment through deliberate, careful steps – is shared by amblers and mountaineers alike. There's an evolutionary component to our enjoyment of lofty views, too. Surveying a large area from a high point allowed our ancestors to scan the horizon for threats. The deep sense of calm we feel is more than admiring a view, it's the satisfaction of our inner hunter-gatherer.

ENDORSE ENJOYMENT OF THE GREAT OUTDOORS BY TELLING YOUR FRIENDS AND FAMILY TO TAKE A HIKE

STRETCHING FROM STUDLAND BAY TO EXMOUTH, THE JURASSIC COAST SPANS 185 MILLION YEARS OF HISTORY

99

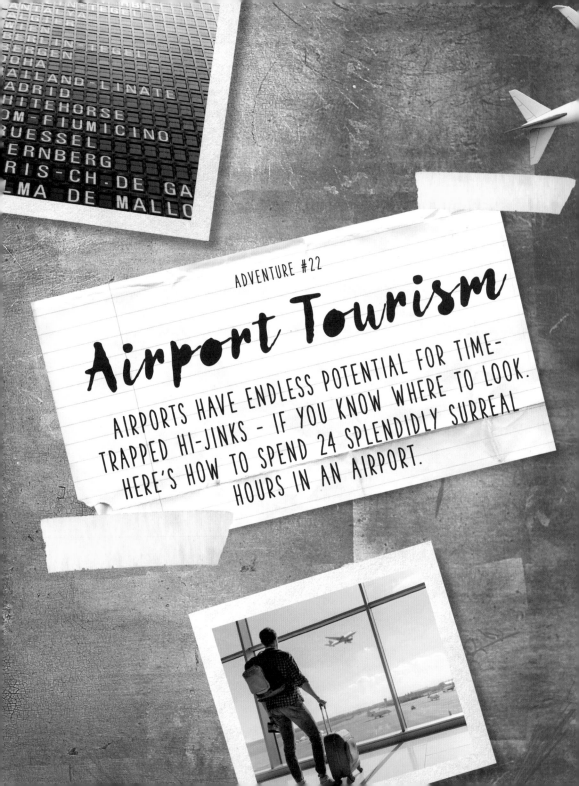

ADVENTURE #22

Airport Tourism

AIRPORTS HAVE ENDLESS POTENTIAL FOR TIME-
TRAPPED HI-JINKS – IF YOU KNOW WHERE TO LOOK.
HERE'S HOW TO SPEND 24 SPLENDIDLY SURREAL
HOURS IN AN AIRPORT.

What you'll need

COMFY CLOTHES & AN AIRLINE-BRANDED EYE-MASK

ABSOLUTELY NO PASSPORT

Instructions

1. PACK A BAG WITH ALL YOU NEED TO GET THROUGH A SLEEPLESS 24 HOURS: NIBBLES, NECK PILLOW, ANYTHING YOU'D BRING ON A LONG-HAUL FLIGHT.

2. TAKE THE SCENIC ROUTE TO THE AIRPORT; NO FLIGHT MEANS NO RUSH.

3. SEE THE SIGHTS, FROM MULTIFAITH CHAPELS TO ARCHITECTURAL ODDITIES.

4. NEXT ENJOY THE FOOD SCENE, WITH BONUS POINTS FOR INAPPROPRIATELY TIMED MEALS (MORNING BEERS OR EVENING ENGLISH BREAKFASTS).

5. GET MISTY-EYED IN ARRIVALS, WATCHING FAMILIES AND LOVERS REUNITE.

COMPLEXITY ★ ★ ★ ★ ★

Case study
Michael Clerizo, Airport Idler

Trundling to Heathrow airport, a sense of liberation washes over me. Unlike my previous journeys to airports, I have not once glanced at my watch. Time doesn't matter.

At 7am, I arrive at Terminal 4. The information desk staff recommend I visit St George's chapel. Embroidered onto the cloth covering the largest altar are three aeroplanes. But my personal vote for the prettiest site at Heathrow is the entry/exit ramp that wraps around Short Stay Car Park 1. Built from concrete and bricks, the sweeping curve of the ramp is as pretty as any French chateau staircase.

An airport is a superb place for watching the world come and go. I observe as people embrace, kiss, cry or yell down their mobile phones: 'I'm here, stupid – where are you?'

At a little after midnight, the show ends. As the food shops close, I stock up on provisions for the night. Inside a display case, the last doughnut is sitting next to an onion bhaji. I haggle and get the doughnut at half-price. Hoping for an invigorating sugar rush, I eat the doughnut. It tastes of onion bhaji.

I decide to push a baggage trolley through the tunnels, and the child in me takes over. I realise that I am reliving a game I played years ago in shopping-mall parking lots. I haven't lost my touch, because I am still able to jump onto the back of the trolley and coast to a gentle stop. I attract the attention of others. A honeymooning couple from Texas, Brad and Amy, who have missed a connecting flight to Italy, have a few goes.

Back on the Piccadilly Line, I experience the perfect ending. I fall asleep.

Pros and Cons

+ Inner child
− Insomnia

WATCH TEARFUL FAMILIES
REUNITE IN THE ARRIVALS AREA;
BLEND IN BY HOLDING A SIGN
BEARING AN INVENTED NAME

Flights of Fancy

Some airports have all the aesthetic appeal of a filing cabinet. Others preen with fabulous architecture and homages to local culture. Take Terminal 4 of Madrid's Barajas Airport, whose bright pylons fade between all the colours of the rainbow. Amsterdam's Schiphol airport harbours a pocket-sized Rijksmuseum. In Kuala Lumpur, there's an indoor rainforest for travellers to explore, allowing them to imagine briefly that they're tramping through the Bornean jungle (instead of waiting for a delayed connection to Melbourne). Incheon is similarly lush, with pine glades and flower gardens. Then there are Miami Airport's therapy dogs, ready to soothe pre-flight nerves with a wet nose and wagging tail. Maybe holidaying at the airport isn't such a bad idea...

LAGOONS, LOOKOUTS AND
JUNGLE GARDENS ARE
THE FUTURE OF AIRPORTS.
FRANKLY, WE'D SETTLE FOR
DECENT WI-FI AND PLENTY
OF PLUG SOCKETS

ADVENTURE #23

Plastic Challenge

DROP THE SODA BOTTLE AND BACK AWAY FROM THE SUPERMARKET CARRIER BAGS! ADAPT YOUR ROUTINE TO SPEND 24 HOURS ENTIRELY PLASTIC-FREE.

What you'll need

REUSABLE ITEMS, LIKE A CANVAS SHOPPING BAG OR COFFEE CUP

Instructions

1. FOR 24 HOURS YOUR CHALLENGE IS TO AVOID PLASTIC, WHOSE MANY (OFTEN UNRECYCLABLE) FORMS ARE A SOURCE OF ENORMOUS WASTE.

2. PLAN AHEAD BY CONSIDERING ONE-USE PLASTICS IN YOUR ROUTINE (PLASTIC BAGS, SODA BOTTLES, DRINKING STRAWS) AND HOW TO AVOID THEM (A CLOTH SHOPPING BAG, REFILLABLE BOTTLE, REQUESTING NO STRAW IN YOUR COCKTAIL...)

3. CHECK ONLINE FOR LOCAL GREEN BUSINESSES, FROM MARKETS TO RESTAURANTS, TO SPRINKLE INTO YOUR DAY.

4. DON'T LET THE ADVENTURE STOP THERE. WRITE TO LOCAL BUSINESSES AND SEE IF YOU CAN CHANGE THE WORLD, ONE PLASTIC BAG AT A TIME.

COMPLEXITY ★ ★ ★ ★ ☆

Case study
Sarah Keid, Mindful Consumer

I avoid single-use plastics wherever possible, but I set out to see if I could last a whole day without *any* plastic. Rolling out of bed, I realise I can't even brush my teeth or wash my hair without using plastic. I make a mental note to invest in a bamboo toothbrush and a shampoo bar, and hope no one smells my breath today.

I'm lucky to live in Byron Bay, one of Australia's most environmentally aware towns, yet plastic is still everywhere. Most local cafes use takeaway coffee cups that contain some sort of plastic, so I bring my own mug to Bayleaf Cafe, which encourages customers to BYO. Munching on a fresh pastry while I wait for my latte, I plan my shopping list.

First up is a trip to the weekly farmers' market, where I load a canvas bag with unpackaged produce. I pass on my usual plastic mesh bag of passionfruit, and ask for no sticky tape when my lettuces are wrapped in butcher's paper. So far, so green.

Forced to forego plastic-packaged feta in my lunchtime salad, I pop into The Source, a plastic-free wholefoods store I've been meaning to check out, to pick up some salad-pimping ingredients. I get a bit excited and purchase enough to outlast an apocalypse.

After work, I meet a friend for a drink – sans plastic straw – before grabbing a falafel wrap (with no plastic bag) to go. It feels good to end the day with a pantry of healthy food and zero plastic use to my name, but keeping up the routine long-term would be tough. Giving it a shot for a day has certainly challenged me to step up my game.

Pros and Cons

+ Saving the planet
+ Mindfulness
– Foregoing daily luxuries

A WICKER BASKET IS VERY ECO-
FRIENDLY; PAIR WITH A BONNET
FOR A DASH OF 18TH-CENTURY
PEASANT CHIC

Plastic Apocalypse

A lot can happen in 450 years: 42 popes; inventions of the telescope, steam locomotive and modern camera; too many wars to accurately count. And 450 years is also roughly the amount of time it takes for a plastic bottle to degrade. Some eco-friendly bioplastics decay more quickly, though others could take a millennium. Single-use plastics rose to ubiquity only in the last few decades, so no one has been able to observe first-hand how long they take to decompose. In a laboratory setting, scientists place plastics in landfill-style environments and measure the CO_2 produced when microbes attack it, to estimate the biodegradation time. But in many landfill sites where garbage is piled high, decomposition would take longer for layers buried deep and starved of air.

SOME CAFES ENCOURAGE
CUSTOMERS TO BRING
THEIR OWN MUG. IF YOURS
DOESN'T, BE THE PERSON
TO START THE TREND

105

ADVENTURE #24

Zero Budget Day Out

SPEND TIME, NOT MONEY! BY IMPOSING A BUDGET OF ZERO ON YOUR DAY, YOU'LL BE FORCED TO GET CREATIVE.

What you'll need

EMPTY POCKETS

BRIMMING IMAGINATION

Instructions

LEAVE CASH AND CREDIT CARDS AT HOME FOR THIS EXPERIMENT IN THRIFT. FOR ONE DAY, YOU'RE OPTING OUT OF CAPITALISM AND NOT SPENDING A SINGLE COIN.

SKIP SHOPPING OR YOUR USUAL BRUNCH AND HUNT OUT FREE GALLERIES INSTEAD. RATHER THAN A MOVIE OR DRINKS WITH FRIENDS, LOOK FOR A FREE COMEDY NIGHT. TAXIS, TRAINS OR BUSES? FORGET IT, YOU'RE WALKING, CYCLING OR CADGING A LIFT WITH FRIENDS.

FOOD AND DRINK REQUIRE THE MOST CREATIVITY. DO YOU DARE CHAT UP STRANGERS TO EAT THEIR CHIPS, CHARM YOUR WAY TO A FREE COFFEE, OR GATECRASH SOMEONE'S PICNIC?

COMPLEXITY ★ ★ ★ ☆ ☆

Case study
Joe Davis, Oxford-Born Budget Traveller

Unburdened by my wallet and with my brother's bike at my disposal, I set off to explore Oxford. I cycle over Magdalen Bridge, watching punts disappear underneath. Next, I slip through the blink-and-you-miss-it hole in the wall to Magdalen Deer Park. It's free for residents and feels miles away from the city.

The best way to see the city for free is by roaming its cobbled streets. After a lap of the skyline's main attraction, the Radcliffe Camera, and a stroll under the Venetian-inspired Bridge of Sighs, I tag along on a free walking tour. I discover hidden blue plaques and a wooden wardrobe-like door that inspired CS Lewis' famous novel. Climbing to the roof of The Varsity Club gives me a view over perfectly square college lawns – a free alternative to the lookout in the University Church of St Mary the Virgin.

All this walking and pub-hopping is hungry work. In desperation, I resort to the next-best-thing-to-free, a discounted supermarket sandwich. A short jaunt away is the perfect picnic spot of Port Meadow, a vast expanse of land dotted with cattle. I complete a short loop along the Thames and grudgingly eat my basic lunch.

Cowley Road is the self-proclaimed 'sunny side of Oxford' and my favourite street in the city. I walk past vibrant street art and inhale smells of every cuisine before heading to record store and coffee shop hybrid Truck Store, to catch a live band for free.

Oxford almost has too much choice for a zero-budget traveller. Having limits in place forces me to deviate from my usual itinerary and discover a new perspective.

Pros and Cons

+ New discoveries
- Hunger pangs
- Beer costs money

Freegan Feasting

The trickiest part of a zero budget day out is filling your stomach. But communities of 'freegans' do it every day, acquiring discarded food for no cost. By rummaging through the bins of restaurants and supermarkets, freegans are using food that would otherwise rot in a landfill site. Their no-waste ideology is underpinned by the desire to reduce their participation in capitalism as far as possible. Many freegans also forage for food that grows wild, and engage in skill swaps with the goal of becoming entirely self-sufficient. If gobbling up food that would otherwise be wasted sounds harmless, it might surprise you that many supermarkets disagree. Some go as far as padlocking trash bins and spoiling food waste by sloshing cleaning products over it.

FREEGAN FOOD LOOKS UNAPPETISING, UNTIL YOU TEAR OPEN THE BAGS TO REVEAL ORGANIC VEGGIES AND THAT EXPENSIVE BRAND OF HUMMUS

109

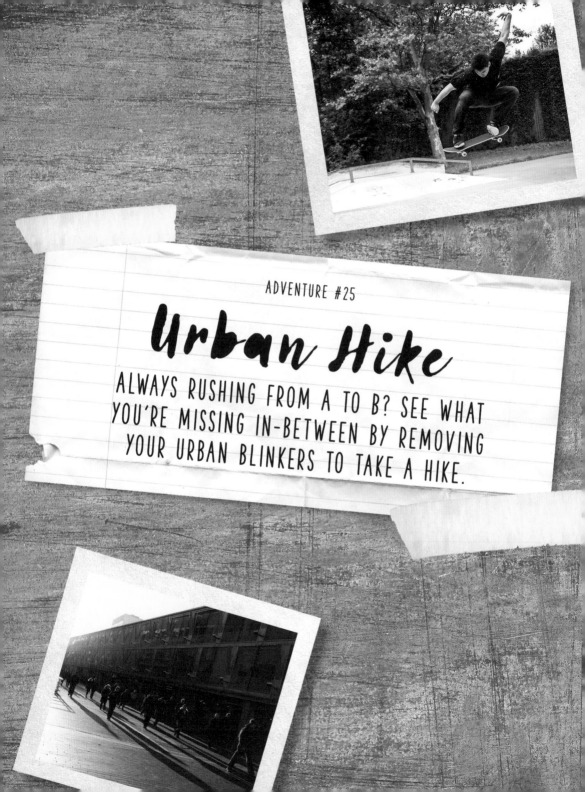

Urban Hike

ALWAYS RUSHING FROM A TO B? SEE WHAT YOU'RE MISSING IN-BETWEEN BY REMOVING YOUR URBAN BLINKERS TO TAKE A HIKE.

What you'll need

ONLINE MAPPING TOOL & SOLID WALKING SHOES

Instructions

1. PICK A LOCAL TRAIN, CAR OR BUS ROUTE WHOSE IN-BETWEEN IS A MYSTERY TO YOU. THE GOAL IS TO HIKE THE JOURNEY, INSTEAD OF ZOOMING THROUGH.

2. RESIST THE TEMPTATION TO CREATE A HIKING ROUTE THROUGH GARDENS AND PARKS. YOU'RE AN URBAN EXPLORER, AND YOUR TREKKING TERRAIN SHOULD BE RESIDENTIAL STREETS, SKATE PARKS AND OTHER URBAN SPACES.

3. DISTANCES CAN BE DECEPTIVE IF YOU'RE USED TO ZIPPING AROUND BY PUBLIC TRANSPORT. USE ONLINE MAP TOOLS TO WORK OUT THE HIKE'S DURATION.

4. PREPARE AS YOU WOULD FOR A WILDERNESS HIKE. BRING WATER AND SNACKS, AND WEAR SUITABLE SHOES. TREKKING POLES MIGHT BE OVERKILL.

COMPLEXITY ★ ☆ ☆ ☆ ☆

Case study
Matt Phillips, North Bank Cyclist

I'm a north of the Thames regular, cycling to work through London's West End and back via Victoria and Chelsea Embankment. While glimpsing the river's south bank, I never experience it, so today I'm hiking 16km between Blackfriars Bridge and Barnes.

Oddly, the first thing that catches my eye is something on the north bank – St Paul's Cathedral. Despite the urge to linger, I stroll westward beneath the iconic Oxo Tower. Although the pavement is buzzing with people, it feels peaceful. Unlike the opposite bank, there is no road hugging the river's edge – pedestrians are king!

Skateboarders find a haven here too, completing their mesmerising tricks in the graffiti-clad space beneath the Southbank Centre, one of the area's best Brutalist buildings. I soon encounter a new face of London, a building boom of gleaming residential skyscrapers. Some are now breathing life into the south bank's most prominent (and derelict) structure: Battersea Power Station. Construction stops at Battersea Park, where I soak up its lush gardens and picturesque lakes.

More footpaths guide me west past riverside pubs – The Ship near Wandsworth Bridge is particularly welcoming. On the quiet backwater of Putney Embankment I find London's spiritual home of rowing, where clubs and boats outnumber cars. Next is a quaint footbridge onto a forested towpath, which follows me for the final kilometres.

My hike has certainly shown me new sides to urban London, and by finishing in nature, with dirt under foot, I also experience a part of the city that feels a world away from my normal stomping (and cycling) grounds.

Pros and Cons

+ Pockets of nature
- Distance between public toilets

7AM SKYPE MEETING, 8AM
BREAKFAST BRAINSTORMING
SESSION, 9AM HIKE ALONG
LONDON'S SOUTH BANK

Brain Trickery

Our minds don't only perceive the world, they create it. Rather than waste precious brain power on sensory perception of a familiar environment – those trees you drive past each day, the shape of your apartment window – your brain colours between the lines.

No wonder, then, that it's so easy to miss interesting details along a familiar route. Our brains' tendency to not only interpret but *create* our reality is why attendees of an event can later recall it in different ways (and eyewitnesses can adamantly point the finger at the wrong suspect of a crime). Optical illusions, where shapes of the same size or colour appear different, work by revealing instances where our brains are creatively interpreting sensory data. All the more reason to slow down and observe what's around you...

URBAN HIKES ARE BEST
AVOIDED IN YOUR LUNCH
HOUR, IN CASE YOU'RE
STRUCK BY THE URGE NOT
TO RETURN

113

ADVENTURE #26

Lend a Hand Locally

LOVE YOUR NEIGHBOURHOOD, DON'T JUST LIVE IN IT. SPARE A DAY FOR VOLUNTEER WORK AND EMERGE AS A MORE MINDFUL CITIZEN.

What you'll need

A WORTHY CAUSE

Instructions

1. SEEK OUT A CHARITY, ENVIRONMENTAL ACTION GROUP, HOME FOR THE ELDERLY OR OTHER NONPROFIT IN NEED OF VOLUNTEERS. DIG AROUND ONLINE FORUMS OR COMMUNITY NOTICEBOARDS, OR SIMPLY ASK AROUND.

2. GOOD WITH ANIMALS, PHYSICALLY STRONG OR GREAT IN THE KITCHEN? PLAY TO YOUR STRENGTHS WHEN CONSIDERING VOLUNTEERING OPPORTUNITIES.

3. FIND OUT IF YOUR CHOSEN CAUSE ACCEPTS CASUAL VOLUNTEERS OR IF THEY WANT A REGULAR COMMITMENT, AND ASK WHAT TRAINING YOU NEED (IF ANY).

4. CARVE OUT A DAY TO VOLUNTEER AND CONSIDER DOING IT REGULARLY.

COMPLEXITY ★ ★ ★ ★ ★

Case study
Sarah Keid, Friend of the Ocean

Mindful of the devastating impact of marine debris on the world's oceans, I often collect rubbish that the tide – or thoughtless beachgoers – deposit on my local beach when I see it. But I've never done a dedicated beach clean-up. Given how much the ocean contributes to my own wellbeing, I figure it's about time I put more effort into returning the favour, so I carve out a sunny afternoon to assist Natalie Woods, co-founder of Australian not-for-profit Clean Coast Collective, on a proper beach clean-up.

Natalie, who runs volunteer-led beach clean-ups around Australia, directs us to the high tide line, where most marine debris tends to end up. I don't expect to find much, but it's not long before we've filled a reusable bag with plastic straws, face wipes, cigarette butts, snack wrappers, and other plastic fragments. While it's deflating to find so much rubbish, I'm surprised to find our mission quite relaxing.

'It might sound a bit gross to go down to the beach to pick up rubbish, but it can actually be really cathartic,' says Natalie. She's not wrong. There's something very meditative about wandering along the beach, watching hermit crabs scuttle out of my path as I scan the sand for things that shouldn't be there. The process also forces me to reflect on the decisions I make as a consumer that can impact the ocean. It's easy to blame irresponsible tourists – or other countries – for making a mess, but we all have a role to play in protecting the environment.

'Every single purchase I make now, I imagine picking it up off the beach,' says Natalie. From now on, I'll be thinking the same way, too.

Pros and Cons

+ Good karma
+ Reducing stress
- Rubbish-related health hazards

Power Of Altruism

Numerous studies – including a British Medical Journal report in 2016 – reveal that volunteer work has a pronounced and long-lasting positive effect on the mental well-being of the volunteer. And since stress is a trigger for a plethora of physical ailments, bodily health is likely to improve, too. Older volunteers in particular have been shown to have lower blood pressure than their non-volunteering counterparts. Altruism can also have a positive effect in other areas of life. Studies by psychology professor Elizabeth Dunn have repeatedly shown that spending cash on others makes us happier than spending it on ourselves.

Next time you cheer yourself up by buying a cinnamon roll, remember you might be even happier if you pass it to the person behind you in the queue.

FROM CLEANING BEACHES TO CUDDLING CATS, VOLUNTEER WORK IS A TWO-WAY STREET THAT BENEFITS THE VOLUNTEER AS MUCH AS THE CAUSE

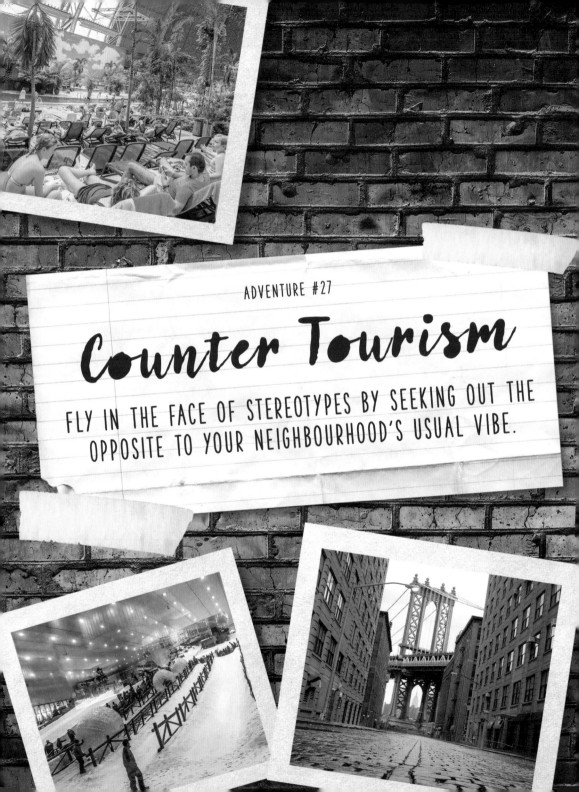

ADVENTURE #27

Counter Tourism

FLY IN THE FACE OF STEREOTYPES BY SEEKING OUT THE OPPOSITE TO YOUR NEIGHBOURHOOD'S USUAL VIBE.

What you'll need

A CONTRARY MINDSET

Instructions

1. WRITE DOWN THREE QUALITIES ASSOCIATED WITH YOUR LOCAL AREA. DON'T THINK TOO HARD: FOOTBALL, RAIN AND LOUD MUSIC ARE FINE FOR MANCHESTER, ENGLAND.

2. DESIGN A DAY THEMED AROUND THE OPPOSITE QUALITIES. IF YOU COME FROM A CITY OF FRENETIC CROWDS AND TRAFFIC, FIND ITS SERENITY. OR IF YOU HAIL FROM A VILLAGE THAT SNOOZES AMONG GREEN HILLS, YOUR QUEST IS TO PARTY UNTIL DAWN.

3. THE MOST ENRICHING WAY TO COMPLETE THIS ADVENTURE IS BY SEEKING OUT A COMMUNITY - BOLLYWOOD DANCE GROUP, VEGAN SUPPER CLUB OR MILLINERY CIRCLE - YOU WOULD NEVER HAVE EXPECTED TO FIND LOCALLY.

COMPLEXITY ★ ★ ★ ★ ☆

Case study
Marika McAdam, Elegance Escapee

Vienna is much like its women – it is beautiful, but it rarely smiles. Mozart wafts through the air with the smell of French perfume and cigarettes. Doormen wear top hats. Even the dogs are designer. The only thing grubby in this impossibly beautiful city is me, and my boots – unfit for the cobblestone streets they traipse.

I decide to find a place where my boots and I belong. I jump on the Straßenbahn until my surroundings no longer make me want to buy clothing I can't afford. After sitting for an hour and a half in a disturbingly clean Straßenbahn, I am still surrounded by buildings on which half-naked angels recline with impossible elegance. But then the tram nears the end of the line…a train station. An ugly one.

I am drawn to a grubby diner nearby where I sip a reasonably priced drink and watch the cast of characters. Women wear make-up more gunky than Gucci and middle-aged men have ambitious ponytails and even more ambitious smiles. There is a real world down here, with litter and loiterers, dreadlocks and drunks, beggars and buskers. As the glamorous folk from the streets descend the escalators to the underground, they shed their rigidly refined elegance; you can virtually hear the sighs as they let out their stomachs. I belong down here, underground and beyond reproach.

But before I am able to celebrate having found a refuge from Viennese beauty, the grimy tunnels of the metro are suddenly transformed into the rich velvet walls of a grandiose opera house and I am plunged once again into a world where I feel underdressed. In this stubbornly sophisticated city, even the buskers play Mozart.

Pros and Cons

+ Rejection of stereotypes
- Insalubrious neighbourhoods
- Identity crisis

VIENNA'S MEDLEY OF
ARCHITECTURAL STYLES:
GOTHIC, BAROQUE AND
GRUNGE (NOT PICTURED)

Being Alternative

Contrariness is a quality we're taught to abandon in childhood. After all, it isn't a good look to whimper for your yellow sweater when only the blue one is clean. Toddlers are experts in contrary behaviour: it's not purely an excuse to have a supermarket meltdown, but a means of exerting control to establish their budding identity. But skilfully timed contrariness is worth taking into adulthood, to occasionally up-end norms we take for granted. Indeed, entertaining an opposite perspective is one of the weapons in a philosopher's toolkit. Philosopher Bertrand Russell explained its importance by writing, 'If an opinion contrary to your own makes you angry, that is a sign that you are subconsciously aware of having no good reason for thinking as you do.'

121

Commute Tourism

COMMUTING TO WORK IS OUR MOST FREQUENTLY UNDERTAKEN (OR ENDURED) JOURNEY - IT'S A WASTE OF TRAVEL NOT TO TURN IT INTO A MINIATURE ADVENTURE.

What you'll need

EARLY START

ALTERNATIVE MODE OF TRANSPORT

Instructions

1. COMMUTE TOURISM INVOLVES ADVENTURE BEFORE YOUR WORKING DAY, SO SET YOUR ALARM AN HOUR OR TWO EARLY (WE PROMISE IT'S WORTH IT).

2. FIND AN INVENTIVE WAY TO GET TO WORK, WHETHER IT'S A BOAT RIDE OR ROLLERSKATING, ALLOWING TIME TO SOAK UP SIGHTS ALONG THE WAY.

3. NO UNUSUAL MODE OF TRANSPORT? TURN YOUR COMMUTE INTO A MINI HOLIDAY INSTEAD: SIGHTSEE IN A CHURCH OR GARDEN YOU NEVER STOP AT, TREAT YOURSELF TO BREAKFAST AT THE MIDWAY POINT, AND SNAP A SELFIE AT A LANDMARK NEAR YOUR OFFICE - #WISHYOUWEREHERE?

COMPLEXITY ★ ☆ ☆ ☆ ☆

123

Case study
Matt Phillips,
Future Frequent Ferryman

Right. It's a simple word with various connotations. This morning it signifies a poignant change of direction. My commute always starts the same way, with a left turn out of my door. It normally takes me and my bicycle through the urban treasures of Kensington and Trafalgar Square. Amazing for sure, but I'm longing for more.

Bike in hand, I take my fateful turn and walk south across Hammersmith Bridge. The beauty of its wrought iron is only eclipsed by the layer of mist dancing in the morning light. I can feel my heart slowing, a novel feeling given my usual commute.

Soon I'm on the Southbank and in my saddle, cycling along the forested towpath to Putney. It's there, at the end of Putney Pier, where my journey truly takes to the water. I join a few others – some in suits, some in lovely dresses, all wearing a perceivable air of tranquillity – for the short wait. Once aboard the ferry, I stay outside on the aft deck as we cruise downstream towards central London.

We cruise majestically past Albert Bridge, the Buddhist Peace Pagoda, Westminster Palace and Big Ben. And perhaps as there is nothing between me and these iconic sights – no streets, no traffic, no honking horns – it feels like I'm experiencing them in a new way, much like viewing exhibits in a remarkable gallery.

As I step reluctantly off the ferry at Blackfriars Pier for the short cycle over the river, I can't help but feel that I've already started my morning with a little holiday. Clearly, the right decision in more ways than one.

Pros and Cons

+ Fresh air
- Motion sickness

SWITCHING YOUR MODE OF TRANSPORT CAN GIVE YOU A FRESH PERSPECTIVE BEFORE YOU ARRIVE AT THE OFFICE

Commuter Conundrums

Who says commuting is dull? Take the case of sisters Heidi Hill and Ashley Benedict, who built a hovercraft out of lawnmower engines and propellers with the help of local aeronautical engineers. The hovercraft enabled them to float across the Mississippi rather than embark on their almost 60km round-trip commute – reliant on a single, traffic-choked bridge – from Cordova, Illinois to Princeton, Iowa. If you aren't able to fashion your own corner-cutting commute, at least know that it could be worse. In 2010, workers snarled up in a 100km tailback on China's National Highway 110 were unable to move their vehicles faster than 1km per hour in a colossal car jam that lasted for 10 days.

HISTORIC SKYLINE DRENCHED IN MORNING SUNLIGHT, OR A GAUNTLET OF CHICKEN SHOPS? FIND THE UNIQUE BEAUTY IN YOUR COMMUTE

125

ADVENTURE #29

Long-Haul Hitchhiking

SEE HOW FAR YOU CAN TRAVEL - TOWNS, REGIONS, EVEN COUNTRIES - PURELY ON THE PERSUASIVE POWERS OF YOUR THUMB.

What you'll need

LARGE PIECE OF CARDBOARD & MARKER PEN

A DESTINATION: THE FURTHER, THE BETTER

HITCHING BUDDY (IT'S SAFER IN A PAIR)

Instructions

HITCHHIKING TO THE NEXT TOWN IS FOR AMATEURS - YOUR GOAL IS TO GET A HECK OF A LOT FURTHER. WHETHER YOU MAKE IT TO AN EXOTIC LOCALE IS UNCERTAIN, BUT YOU'RE GUARANTEED AN INTERESTING JOURNEY...

1. HEAD TO THE HIGHWAY ARMED WITH CARDBOARD, A BACKPACK AND A BUDDY.

2. WRITE THE NAME OF A DREAM DESTINATION ON YOUR SIGN, WHETHER IT'S NYC OR THE BAHAMAS.

3. STICK YOUR THUMB OUT AND WAIT FOR DESTINY TO HONK ITS HORN.

COMPLEXITY ★ ★ ★ ★ ★

Case study
Jeremy Moon,
Cross-Continent Hitcher

I've been standing in the hot sun in Teotihuacan, Mexico with my thumb out for about 20 minutes. My sign says 'SYDNEY' but I'll be happy to go any place that has shade or cold beer (preferably both).

Every car that zooms past is full of evil, selfish people who should be taking pity on me. I'm in a country where I don't speak the language and I'm trying to hitchhike to a city that's on another continent. Hang on, that nice green van is stopping. I'm so happy I don't even notice it's full of people in green uniforms all holding large guns.

'Don't you know that hitchhiking in this country is a shootable offence?' yells one of the soldiers. (Remember, I don't speak the local language, so I'm really just guessing). But I do understand a word from the next sentence. '*Identificación*!' comes out loud and clear.

I hand over my passport and feel relief rush through me as he smiles and then laughs (I really should change that photo). He barks a command and two of the soldiers jump down, grab my pack and fling it into the back of their truck, then proceed to do the same with me. The truck pulls away and my passport is still being passed around the soldiers, who are now either in hysterics or attempting to talk to me in English. After about 30 minutes of bouncing and swerving we grind to a halt and my pack and I are tossed out into the world again. Expecting the worst – a firing squad or a Mexican prison – I realise I've been dropped in front of Purisima station, on the outskirts of Mexico city. The soldier with the loud voice gives me a wave and points towards the metro…

Pros and Cons
+ Free ride
– Fearsome firearms
– Butt of jokes

A CLEARLY WRITTEN SIGN IS ESSENTIAL, AN AIR OF WEARINESS AND DEFEAT IS OPTIONAL

Slight Hitch

For the impoverished 'Okies' depicted in John Steinbeck's *Grapes of Wrath*, hitchhiking was the only way to travel across the US during the Great Depression of the 1930s. During the 1950s, it was the preferred method of transport for beat writers such as Jack Kerouac, Allen Ginsberg and William S. Burroughs, who preferred to spend money on alcohol and typewriting tape. During the 1970s hitchhiking was synonymous with freewheeling hippies. Today it may be considered an ecological choice, but it has declined in popularity due to increased awareness of the associated dangers. Die-hard hitchhikers are still out there. In 1994 Alexey Vorov, president of the St Petersburg Autostop League (PASL), hitchhiked around the world by plane, boat and car.

GET USED TO THE SIGHT OF CHUCKLING DRIVERS IF YOU'RE HITCHING TO A DRAMATICALLY DISTANT LOCALE

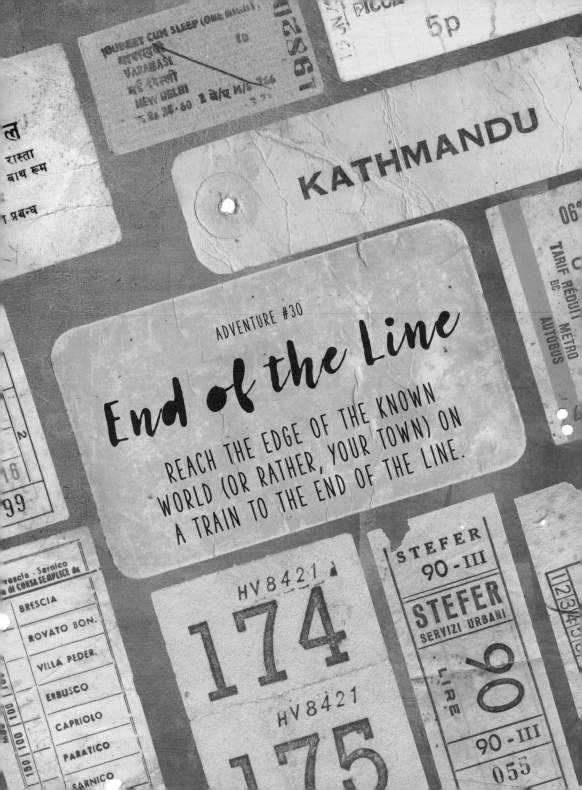

KATHMANDU

ADVENTURE #30

End of the Line

REACH THE EDGE OF THE KNOWN
WORLD (OR RATHER, YOUR TOWN) ON
A TRAIN TO THE END OF THE LINE.

What you'll need

A LOCAL TRAIN WITH A FAR-FLUNG FINAL STATION

Instructions

1. ARRIVING AT THE END OF THE LINE IS USUALLY THE UNFORTUNATE RESULT OF A DRUNKEN SNOOZE ON THE NIGHT TRAIN. THIS TIME, DO IT DELIBERATELY.

2. TAKE A SUBURBAN TRAIN OUT OF THE CITY AND TRAVEL TO THE VERY END OF THE LINE.

3. IF POSSIBLE, FIND A PLACE TO STAY THE NIGHT FOR A MORE THOROUGH INVESTIGATION OF THIS UNKNOWN TERRAIN.

COMPLEXITY ★ ☆ ☆ ☆ ☆

Case study
Rachael Antony, Roaming Filmmaker

Great journeys always seem to entail early rising, so in keeping with the tradition of the explorers who went before us we dutifully set our alarm clocks. With sleepy eyes and fuzzy heads Janet, Dave and I approached Melbourne's Flinders Street train station at 7.30am the next day. Our goal is to travel to the end of the line – the intriguingly named Stony Point – and make a film, the details and motivations of which are unclear.

We take the regular train as far as it will go, then change to another, less frequent diesel version and chug-chug our way to the end of the line. We stop at the sole sign of civilisation, a small general store, where we order a hot cup of tea, debate the relative 'stoniness' of Stony Point ('I've seen stonier,' says Dave, thoughtfully) and wait for the morning fog to clear from the sea.

Our wanderings take us to a bleak and lonely seascape where we improvise an Ingmar Bergman-inspired exchange between Dave and Janet, punctuated with intense looks and 'stony' silences, followed by a rather incomprehensible love story between Janet and the beanbag. Heading off, we come across a spooky, seemingly desolate military base before finding a nature reserve where we rest – Dave and I on the emerald grass, Janet on her beanbag – in a sunny hollow and watch butterflies.

Drowsy from the afternoon sun, Janet dozes on the train back to the urban jungle, while Dave and I muse on the end of the line and the world we found there.

'But where was the point?' I say. David looks into my eyes, stroking an imaginary beard that lends him an air of wisdom. 'There is no point,' he replies. 'It just is.'

Pros and Cons

+ Thrill of discovery
- Nagging sense of futility

World's End

In 1492 Christopher Columbus took a boat to the end of the line. At the time, much of the Western world had accepted a rather eccentric theory that the world was spherical, but some sceptics (and the Catholic Church) were clinging to the established truth: the world was flat and Christopher Columbus was going to sail right off the end of it (thus proving rather definitively that 'pride comes before a fall'). Columbus got lucky – the world was round – but he missed his intended destination (Asia) by a continent or two, winding up instead in the Americas. The native inhabitants were not so lucky, as the arrival of Columbus and his pals resulted in the destruction of life as they had known it. The lesson to be learnt? A voyage to the end of the line, while inspiring and romantic, can have dangerous and unintended consequences.

133

Street Art Odyssey

WHETHER YOUR TOWN IS BLESSED WITH TOWERING MURALS OR SCRAPPY GRAFFITI, STREET ART CAN UNLOCK ITS HIDDEN LIFE.

What you'll need

WALKING SHOES

DISCERNING EYE

Instructions

1. IF YOUR HOME CITY IS KNOWN FOR AMAZING PUBLIC ART - LIKE MELBOURNE, BELFAST OR LOS ANGELES - JOIN A STREET ART TOUR AND LET THE PROS DIVULGE THE STREETS' SECRETS.

2. IF THE RATTLING OF SPRAY CANS IS A FAIRLY COMMON SOUNDTRACK IN YOUR HOME CITY BUT YOU DON'T KNOW WHERE TO START, DOWNLOAD AN APP LIKE HTTP://GEOSTREETART.COM, WHICH HAS UPDATED MAPS OF STREET ART LOCATIONS.

3. TREAT EVERY PIECE OF STREET ART AS IF YOU ARE SEEING IT INSIDE THE LOUVRE. WHAT'S THE ARTIST'S INTENTION, AND HOW DOES IT MAKE YOU FEEL?

COMPLEXITY ★ ★ ★ ★ ★

Case study
Tim Richards, Street Art Addict

As I stand on Flinders Street, I'm surrounded by major landmarks. Federation Square is behind me, Flinders Street Station to the left, the Melbourne Cricket Ground to my right. But I'm looking for something grittier: Melbourne's famous street art. Its epicentre is Hosier Lane, the cobblestone laneway in front of me.

There are always tourists walking its length, photographing the splendour on its walls. Every type of street art is here, including tags, stencils and paste-ups; but the laneway is best-known for its murals, bold depictions of characters that pop from the walls. All will eventually be covered by new art. Even my long-standing favourite, a colourful depiction of the Hindu god Ganesha, has now vanished. But its ephemeral nature is key to such art's appeal.

From Hosier I turn into Rutledge Lane, a narrower horseshoe-shaped alley which seems awash with paint. The art here is less crowd-pleasing but just as powerful, with tags and political messages joining works such as a giant painting of a fruit bat.

Further east, quieter AC/DC Lane (named for the Aussie rock band) is another treasure trove. As the laneway bends to become Duckboard Place, I spot a rat image which might have been rendered by the notorious Banksy. But who knows?

My final stop is a subversive blaze of colour. Union Lane runs off Bourke Street Mall, the city's shopping hub. Forget murals: this is a sea of tags, those cryptic signatures that mark street artists' territory. Somehow they seem a symbol of Melbourne's complexity, a multitude of secrets hidden in an alleyway at its heart.

Pros and Cons

+ Ever-changing art
- Strong paint smell

STREET ARTISTS SUCH AS ERNEST ZACHAREVIC DEVISE SURREAL COMBINATIONS OF SUBJECT AND CANVAS, OFTEN AS WRY COMMENTARY ON URBAN LIFE

Giants of Graffiti

Street art has existed ever since humans could clutch a rock well enough to carve an inscription. In 1920s NYC and Latin America, train carriages daubed with territorial doodles were calling cards among gangs. Nowadays walls covered in initials and scrawls are often training grounds for street art's future greats, who finesse their command of the can from lines to detailed murals. And it's not all paint cans: street artists use mixed media and a plethora of techniques. Portuguese artist Vhils scratches away dirt and old paint to create huge portraits, Buenos Aires-based Jaz employs tar and gasoline. Lithuanian artist Ernest Zacharevic created an arresting piece in Kuala Lumpur depicting children attacking a blazing school bus. His materials? Paint, and half a repurposed bus.

THERE ARE NO BARRIERS TO ACCESS STREET ART, ALLOWING ARTWORK TO BE PUBLICLY ADMIRED, REVILED OR PAINTED OVER

Movie Magic

GET READY FOR YOUR CLOSE-UP... FIND THE NEAREST FILMING LOCATION AND RECREATE SOME ICONIC MOVIE MOMENTS.

What you'll need

MOVIE KNOWLEDGE

CAMERA

RED CARPET (OPTIONAL)

Instructions

THINK OF A MOVIE OR TV SERIES FILMED OR SET CLOSE BY, AND SEEK OUT ITS LOCATION. BETTER YET, BRING A CAMERA AND AN ACCOMPLICE SO YOU CAN RECREATE THE MOST FAMOUS SCENES.

IF SCREENWRITERS ARE YET TO IMMORTALISE YOUR TOWN, USE A LITTLE ARTISTIC LICENCE. CAN YOU REPLICATE CASABLANCA AT A TRAIN STATION, TRON AT YOUR LOCAL LASER-TAG OR THE LION KING USING THE STAR POWER OF YOUR NEIGHBOUR'S CATS?

COMPLEXITY ★ ★ ★ ★ ★

Case study
Lucy Corne, Sports Movie Convert

I'm not much of a sports movie fan, but then *Invictus* was much more than a sports movie. And just as the film sought to tell a chapter of South African history through sport, so did I seek to see the city I've called home for seven years through a sport that its people revere: rugby.

My quest begins with a curve ball. I want to start at the spot where Morgan Freeman's Nelson Mandela first greets the Springboks, handing over a copy of the poem that lends its title to the movie. After some internet sleuthing, I work out where filming took place and head for the edge of Tokai Forest. Alas, I arrive to realise that movies aren't always filmed in publicly accessible places and am turned away by a surly security guard. Content that I at least ventured to this corner of the city, I head for the main event.

Newlands Stadium is home to Cape Town's rugby union club and the site of South Africa's 1995 opening World Cup win over Australia – both on- and off-screen. It's a neighbourhood I visit often, but I've never set foot in the stadium. A pre-booked tour takes me through the stands and private boxes, but it's the pitch I'm really here for. I stand on the halfway line and soak up the silence. While it's Matt Damon I'm picturing, it's not the fact that this was a movie location that inspires – it's the real events that prompted the film.

I close my eyes to the views of Table Mountain and try to comprehend how right here, sport played its part in helping to dismantle the dreaded apartheid regime.

Pros and Cons

+ Celebrity fever
- Inaccessible sites
- No actual celebrities

UNLEASH YOUR INNER MOVIE
DIRECTOR BY DONNING BIG
SUNGLASSES WHILE YOU TOUR
FILMING LOCATIONS

Here Be Dragons

Filming locations for fantasy TV series *Game of Thrones*, like the ramparts of Dubrovnik and Northern Ireland's enigmatic cliffs, have received a tourism stampede. But both places have a disappointing lack of dragons. If only they'd filmed the series in Slovenia, where real-life dragons are commonplace. Dragons grace bridges and art across this central European country. And in Postojna, embryonic 'dragons' are a major attraction. Postojna's olm, a cave-dwelling amphibian found nowhere else on Earth, was initially believed to be a baby dragon. The truth may be even stranger. Scientists remain dumbfounded about how these pale, blind critters thrive: their breeding patterns are a mystery and they can survive for decades without eating.

FANCY HAVING AN ANITA
EKBERG MOMENT IN
ROME'S TREVI FOUNTAIN?
SADLY LOCAL AUTHORITIES
TAKE A DIM VIEW OF LA
DOLCE VITA RECREATIONS

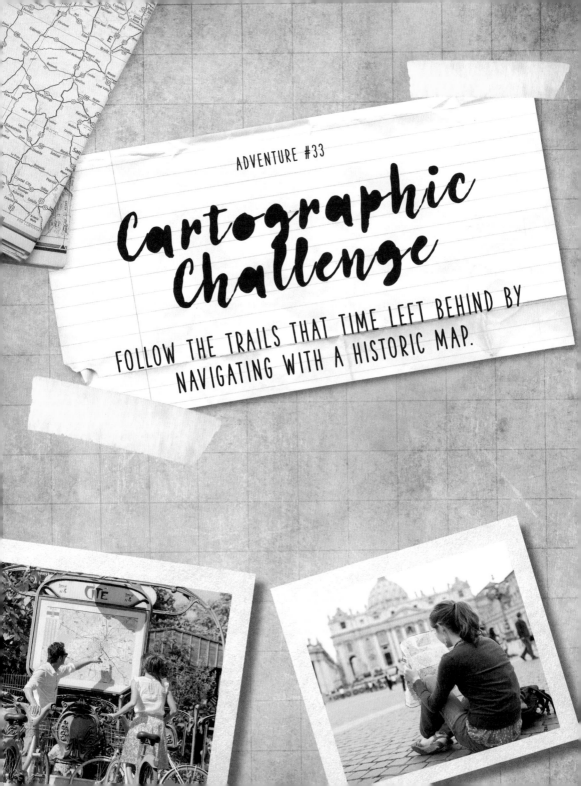

ADVENTURE #33

Cartographic Challenge

FOLLOW THE TRAILS THAT TIME LEFT BEHIND BY NAVIGATING WITH A HISTORIC MAP.

What you'll need

OUTDATED MAP

A DASH OF NOSTALGIA

Instructions

1. GET YOUR HANDS ON AN OLD MAP OF YOUR AREA BY SCOURING THE WEB OR A LOCAL LIBRARY.

2. IF YOU KNOW THE HISTORY OF YOUR NEIGHBOURHOOD, FIND A MAP ISSUED BEFORE A MAJOR BUILDING PROJECT OR KEY EVENT IN YOUR HOMETOWN'S HISTORY.

3. NAVIGATE AROUND TOWN USING ONLY THE OLD MAP, AND RUMINATE ON HOW YOUR 'HOOD HAS CHANGED OVER THE YEARS.

COMPLEXITY **★ ★ ★ ★ ★**

Case study
Belinda Dixon,
Cartographic Time Traveller

I'm bumping along on the bus, strangely excited about a ride into town. I'm studying a batch of maps showing my city through the eras, from 1809 to present day. What stories will they tell of continuity and change?

In 1896 my home was surrounded by fields. Today cafes and pubs flash by. Convenience or green spaces, which would I prefer? We cruise down a three-lane highway that my 1930s map reveals was a railway line; I can almost smell the steam.

In the city centre, those old maps fail: the streets here were re-routed after WWII bombing. Roads that had evolved into a spider's web were replaced by a grid.

Up to the sea-backed headland of Plymouth Hoe. A 1919 map shows jaunty Promenade Pier; a pleasure palace destroyed by bombing raids. Nearby a graceful, cream-and-blue Art Deco lido still sweeps from the shore. Missing from my early maps, it was only built in 1935. Today, sunshine ensures it's crowded with laughing swimmers; past meets present in playful style. At Fishers Nose (making an 1809 cartographic appearance) I spot ranks of rods and lines – some things never change.

Onwards to Plymouth's historic Barbican, where half-timbered houses and cobbled lanes echo the ancient street plan. At the Mayflower Steps, the departure point of America's Pilgrim Fathers in 1620, the Union Jack flutters by the Stars and Stripes, and ferries prepare to set sail. Perhaps every town has these: places of arrivals and departures, where past meets present and even old maps can show you the way.

Pros and Cons

+ Sense of continuity
– Wistfulness

USE AN OUTDATED MAP TO FEEL
THE PULSE OF YOUR TOWN'S
GLORY DAYS (OR SEEDY PAST)

AN ART-DECO TREASURE
TO INSPIRE WISTFUL
WANDERING: THE
1935-BUILT TINSIDE POOL
IN PLYMOUTH, ENGLAND

Monster Maps

If you've ever blown dust from a historic map, you've seen monsters peering from the parchment. Medieval cartographers drew a menagerie of mythical beasts on maps: mermaids, octopi the size of continents, and serpents dragging ships to doom. In part, these marine fiends evoked the ocean's destructive power; but many such drawings were an earnest guess at the creatures that might reside in the sea. Land animals were believed to have a marine equivalent – a theory that dates to Pliny the Elder's 37-volume opus *Natural History* – so artists decorated maps with oceanic pigs, waterbound canines and other hybrid animals. Plus, sailors didn't usually return with picture-perfect recall of the walruses and narwhals they spotted, thereby transforming them into grotesque beasts.

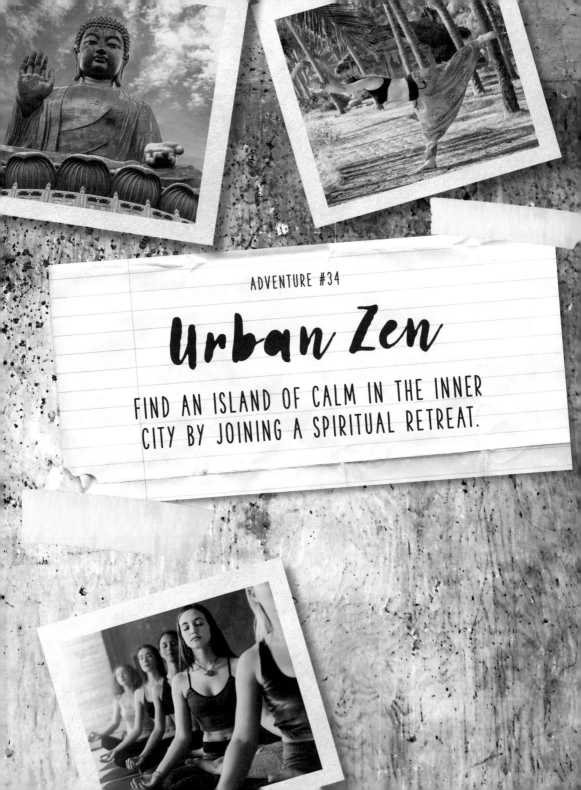

ADVENTURE #34

Urban Zen

FIND AN ISLAND OF CALM IN THE INNER
CITY BY JOINING A SPIRITUAL RETREAT.

What you'll need

GOOD ATTENTION SPAN

MEDITATION GROUP

Instructions

RETREAT FROM THE INNER-CITY PRESSURE COOKER. ALMOST ALL SIZEABLE TOWNS AND CITIES HAVE SPIRITUAL CENTRES AND MEDITATION GROUPS, AND MANY OF THEM WELCOME CURIOUS BEGINNERS.

BUDDHIST, HINDU AND MEDITATIVE KABBALAH GROUPS ARE COMMON, WHILE CATHOLICS INSPIRED BY THE SPIRITUALITY OF ST IGNATIUS OF LOYOLA ORGANISE 'SILENT RETREATS' IN WHICH PARTICIPANTS PONDER AND PRAY IN COMPLETE SILENCE FOR A DAY OR MORE. RESEARCH WHETHER THERE ARE ANY RETREAT CENTRES OR MEDITATION SCHOOLS NEAR YOU AND TAKE YOUR FIRST STEPS TOWARDS ENLIGHTENMENT.

COMPLEXITY ★ ★ ★ ★ ★

Case study
Christina Webb, Seeker of Calm

Amidst the weekend crowds on the London Underground, I'm looking quite the opposite of calm. I'm tired, overheated and worrying that my destination, a meditative yoga day retreat, will be full of hyper-extending yogis folding themselves in two. And while I have been on a retreat before, I've never experienced a full day of practise.

When I arrive at the Buddhist centre in London, I'm greeted with smiles and met with an immediate sense of calm. I peek into the meditation spaces while people trickle inside. The rooms are minimalistic, with dimmed lighting and shrines. There is a community atmosphere as we help ourselves in the kitchen and drink tea made from fresh mint that someone picked from their garden this morning.

In the studio, mats are laid out in a semi-circle. My earlier fears ease off as I see that we are all ages, shapes and abilities. We start with meditation, allowing me to push past my regular shallow breathing. Our focus is helped with guided meditation and pauses for discussion – useful for novices. We break to chat over juicy watermelon.

I realise this is the longest I've spent practising, but it's not overwhelming – the full day slows our pace. We look at adjustments to each pose in detail, collectively looking at anatomical alignment to help with tight hamstrings or lower back pain.

As I walk out into the busy street I feel physically stronger and less distracted by the hustle and bustle. I've realised the importance of focusing on my body and slowing down for a day, and I didn't even have to leave the city.

Pros and Cons

+ Confidence
+ New friends
- Distant hum of traffic

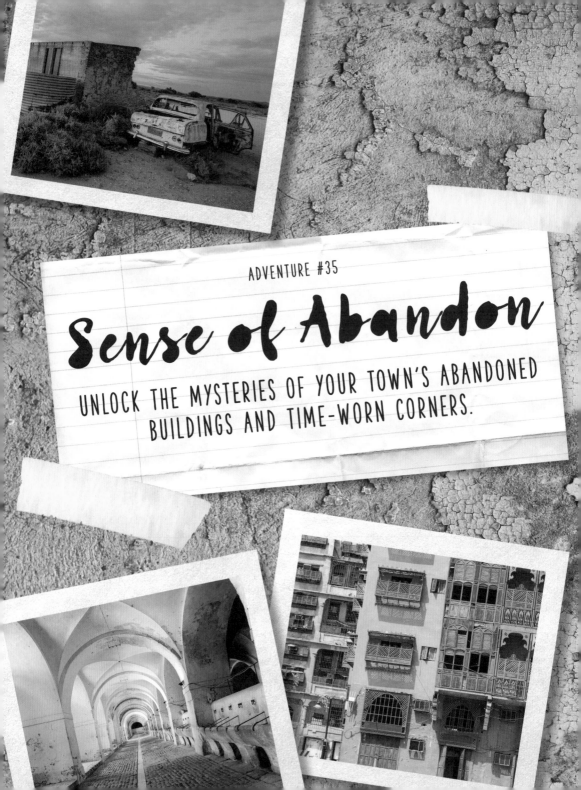

Sense of Abandon

UNLOCK THE MYSTERIES OF YOUR TOWN'S ABANDONED BUILDINGS AND TIME-WORN CORNERS.

What you'll need

A NEW DEFINITION OF BEAUTY

Instructions

CRUMBLING HOUSES, EMPTY FACTORIES, OVERGROWN PARKLAND...EVERY TOWN HAS UNTENDED CORNERS THAT GUARD THE SECRETS OF ITS PAST LIFE.

IN THIS ADVENTURE, YOUR AIM IS TO FIND THE BEAUTY IN ABANDONED PLACES. THEY MIGHT INCLUDE SHUTTERED FACTORIES, OLD CEMETERIES, WEATHER-BEATEN STATUES AND CONDEMNED APARTMENT BLOCKS.

FOR SAFETY REASONS, WE STRONGLY ADVISE AGAINST EXPLORING THE INTERIOR OF ABANDONED STRUCTURES. ALWAYS HEED WARNING SIGNS THAT FENCE OFF DERELICT AREAS.

COMPLEXITY ★★★★★

Case study
Luke Waterson, Brutalism Aficionado

In Bratislava, as with other former Eastern Bloc cities, visitors might stay in the attractive Old Town but a fraction of citizens live there: they inhabit the less lovely, largely Communist-constructed surrounds. Under Communism, historic centres were abandoned (too bourgeois) in favour of the proletariat-friendly breezeblock periphery.

These concrete outskirts might be lived in, but now they have become the neglected neighbourhoods, as main roads or railways deliver people speedily to central, more aesthetically pleasing areas. A regime change casts a profound feel of dereliction. Around Bratislava such structures crouch like ghosts, seen but unseen, the land around them untended. Others whoosh through these outskirts; I like to walk.

Bratislava boasts hundreds of statues, often testament to brazen Communist design. These sculptures lead you on a trail through unkempt outer Bratislava: a swing with a boulder strapped to it in scenic-but-scruffy Horský Park, and a blue and salmon-pink fountain where the tower blocks of Rača abut rolling vineyards.

In fields outside an out-of-town retail park in Petržalka, a WWII bunker (now refurbished) contains insightful displays about its history. Overlooked fortifications also riddle Devínska Kobyla, a wooded massif rising out of Bratislava's otherwise bland western suburbs: many were Communist-era border defences.

There is something ominous about concrete mementos of bygone times, shaken by the rumble of traffic. But there is intrigue, too. Many of these constructions stand forgotten in edgelands, neither city nor countryside, exuding their surreal enigma.

Pros and Cons

+ Unchampioned urban beauty
- Bad graffiti

NOTE THAT A GREAT MANY
HORROR MOVIES BEGIN WITH
CAREFREE TEENS FROLICKING IN
SIGHT OF AN ABANDONED CABIN

Urban Decay

'Urban explorers' laugh in the face of trespassing laws and travel insurance. Urban exploration involves breaking, sneaking or crawling into an abandoned man-made structure, be it an old quarry, disused factory or sewer; bonus points for high radiation levels, like the ghost town of Pripyat, abandoned after 1986's Chernobyl disaster. A much more challenging Ukrainian urban exploration site is in Odessa. Its catacombs are the world's largest, 2500km of tunnels spidering beneath the city. Initially carved out as limestone mines, the tunnels were hiding grounds for WWII partisan fighters. In the 1960s, the Poisk ('search') speleological club set about mapping the labyrinth beneath Odessa. Their services are now called on when amateur urban explorers get lost...

THE FERRIS WHEEL IN
PRIPYAT, A GHOST TOWN
EVACUATED AFTER THE
CHERNOBYL NUCLEAR
DISASTER, IS NOW AN
EERIE TOURIST CURIOSITY

Vintage Travel

EVER CONSIDERED TRAVEL BY HORSE-AND-CARRIAGE OR UNICYCLE? REKINDLE THE ROMANCE OF A BYGONE ERA ABOARD AN OUTMODED MEANS OF TRANSPORT.

What you'll need

ACCESS TO AN OUTDATED FORM OF TRANSPORT (ESSENTIAL)

PERIOD COSTUME (OPTIONAL)

Instructions

THIS ADVENTURE TRANSPORTS YOU TO THE DAYS OF BONE-RATTLING CARRIAGES OR RIVER-SPLASHED GONDOLA RIDES...ALL WHILE LOOKING VINTAGE FABULOUS.

SO, WHAT'S AVAILABLE? IF YOUR BIKE SHOP HAS A UNICYCLE AROUND THE BACK, OR A FRIEND WITH ACCESS TO THEATRE PROPS CAN LEND YOU A SEDAN CHAIR, AN ADVENTURE IN NOSTALGIC TRANSPORT IS YOURS.

OTHERWISE, ENTER TOURIST TERRITORY. HAIL AN OLD-SCHOOL TRISHAW OR SPLURGE ON A CARRIAGE RIDE. WHATEVER YOU CHOOSE, DRESS APPROPRIATELY: WE FIND A BOATER HAT OR LONG GLOVES SUIT MOST VINTAGE MODES OF TRAVEL.

COMPLEXITY ★ ★ ★ ★ ★

Case study
Sally Dillon, Nostalgic Pedaller

I came late to the world of penny-farthing cycling. More than a century late, in fact. When everyone else was discovering bicycles with 24 speeds, suspension and lightweight alloy frames, I was revelling in the old-fashioned delights of the highwheel bicycle. One speed, no brakes, and a solid rubber tyre on a 50-inch (1.3m) wheel.

Togged up in full Victorian costume, my husband, Peter, and I set off through the backstreets high atop our penny-farthings to meet some friends for coffee. We are in Melbourne, where the graceful gardens and tree-lined streets lend themselves perfectly to such period re-creations. Cruising towards the traffic lights at St Kilda Rd, we wonder what those who monitor the traffic cameras will make of the scene.

We glide down the peaceful side streets of South Melbourne. Ivy trails over high brick fences that protect residents from the gaze of passers-by – except those passers-by who are mounted 6ft (1.8m) above the ground on a penny-farthing. A look of bewilderment replaces passion on the faces of the couple we spot *in flagrante delicto* in their backyard.

We reach South Melbourne Market, and compose our faces into casual expressions as we ride past the cafes. Families turn to point and stare, trendy young things pretend to ignore us, and middle-aged men laugh at their cleverness in asking, 'How's the weather up there?' Such are the trials of committed Victorian poseurs: the stares, the inane comments, and the blank looks of those who don't want to lower themselves by smiling at the spectacle. We lock our bicycles to a lamppost and sit down to enjoy our coffee. What a way to travel. What a way to arrive.

Pros and Cons

+ Alternate reality
– Dreary modern traffic rules

MELAKA AND GEORGE TOWN IN
MALAYSIA ARE TRISHAW HEAVEN,
MANY OF THEM DRAPED WITH
FLOWERS AND FAIRY LIGHTS

Gentleman Globetrotters

The joys and tribulations of vintage travel are nicely evoked in Gustav Temple and Vic Darkwood's 'travel memoir' *Around the World in Eighty Martinis*. This comic tome documents how two chaps take on a wager to travel the globe, crossing all five continents and using a different form of transport for every stage of the journey. Having travelled by yak, balloon and hovercraft (wherein they overcome space and storage difficulties by strapping their trusty butler to the roof racks), they cross the Congo in a sedan chair borne by 'four men in training for the forthcoming Commonwealth Games'. Alas, their passage is brought to a standstill when the pair are kidnapped by gorillas.

PENNY-FARTHING BICYCLES:
COMMON UNTIL THE LATE
19TH CENTURY AND WELL
OVERDUE FOR A COMEBACK

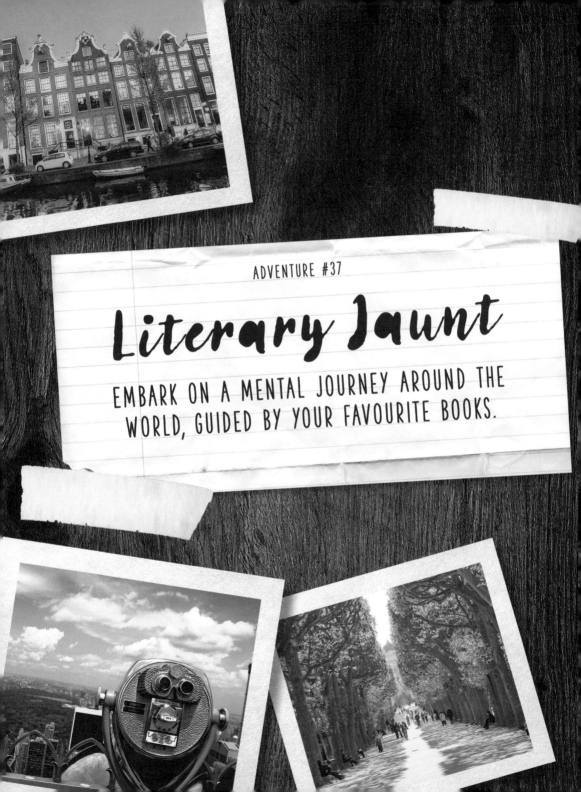

Literary Jaunt

EMBARK ON A MENTAL JOURNEY AROUND THE WORLD, GUIDED BY YOUR FAVOURITE BOOKS.

What you'll need

BULGING BOOKSHELF

Instructions

1. PICK THE FIRST BOOK ON THE TOP-HAND LEFT CORNER OF YOUR BOOKSHELF. THIS IS THE STARTING POINT OF YOUR LITERARY JOURNEY AROUND THE WORLD. READ THE BOOK UNTIL YOU FIND A REFERENCE TO A COUNTRY.

2. SELECT A SECOND BOOK, EITHER THEMED OR SET IN THAT COUNTRY (ALLOWING AS MUCH WIGGLE-ROOM AS REQUIRED) AND BEGIN READING.

3. REPEAT THE PROCESS WHEN YOU SEE A MENTION OF A NEW COUNTRY.

4. YOUR AIM IS EITHER TO RETURN TO THE COUNTRY IN WHICH YOU BEGAN IN THE SPACE OF 10 BOOKS, OR TO MAKE IT ALL THE WAY AROUND THE GLOBE.

COMPLEXITY ★ ★ ★ ★ ☆

Case study
David Prater, Page-Turning Globetrotter

I begin my journey with James Joyce's *A Portrait of the Artist as a Young Man*. My object is to circumnavigate the world and return to Ireland within 10 books. I settle into an armchair, thinking it might be hundreds of pages before I receive a hint about my next stop. Not so: on page five is a reference to the Mozambique Channel.

For my next book, I settle on Craig Werner's *A Change is Gonna Come*, a history of African-American music. Close enough. I start reading, and on the sixth line of the first page I receive my next destination: Vietnam.

From Neil Sheehan's *Two Cities: Hanoi and Saigon* it was a short and perhaps predictable step to France, and Jean Genet's *Our Lady of the Flowers*. This sent me ricocheting across Europe to Germany, courtesy of Günter Grass' *Local Anaesthetic*, whose first page directed me to Alexandria, Egypt. My flight route was beginning to look like a child's drawing – a series of red lines scribbled across the globe. Would I make it back to Ireland in time for tea?

My fate ends up in the hands of Captain Cook, whose *Journals* furnish me with a chance to island-hop to Tahiti, and to Bengt and Marie-Thérèse Danielsson's impassioned history of nuclear testing in the Pacific, *Moruroa, Mon Amour*. They promptly send me to England. Nine books down, and I'm almost back where I started.

Unfortunately, the next book on my shelf by an Englishman is Thomas Hardy's *Jude the Obscure*, in whose Wessex setting I while away the rest of the afternoon. I never make it back to Dublin, but I did manage to see quite a bit of the world.

Pros and Cons

+ Luxuriating in literature
– Pangs of wanderlust

A TRUE BOOKWORM CAN DISCERN THE FUSTY ODOUR OF A SECONDHAND BOOK SHOP FROM MILES AWAY

TRANSPORT YOUR BRAIN TO TUSCANY BY READING NOVELS SET IN THIS STORIED CITY...THEN TRY TO RESIST BUYING A PLANE TICKET

Bodice-Rippers

To Victorian doctors, enthusiasm for literature was highly dangerous – particularly for women. Novels were believed to be a moral risk and a physical danger to the female body. Back in the bad old days, women's wombs were thought to leap around their bodies causing weakness (coincidentally, these were the same days in which it was customary for women to wear breath-constricting corsets). Ghost stories and romances were thought especially risky for the female constitution; luckily medical science outpaced superstition. These days, neuroscientists investigate the phenomenon whereby readers become so immersed in a book that they forget their surroundings. They've learned that the genres most likely to engross readers are, as Victorian doctors feared, ghost stories and romances.

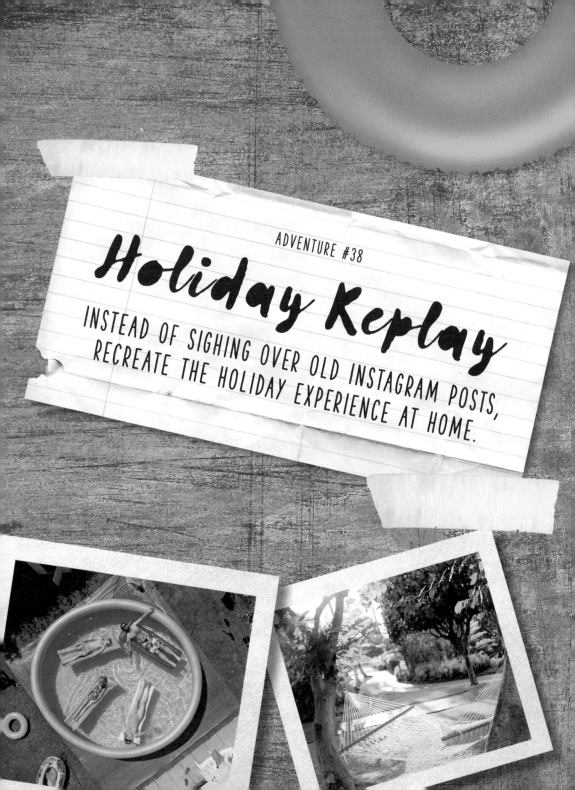

ADVENTURE #38

Holiday Replay

INSTEAD OF SIGHING OVER OLD INSTAGRAM POSTS, RECREATE THE HOLIDAY EXPERIENCE AT HOME.

What you'll need

ROSE-TINTED GLASSES

FOND MEMORIES OF A HOLIDAY

POETIC LICENCE

Instructions

IF YOU COULD TIME-TRAVEL TO THE LOCATION OF A PREVIOUS HOLIDAY, WHERE WOULD IT BE AND WHAT WOULD YOU BE DOING? YOUR CHALLENGE IS TO RECREATE THE SIGHTS, SOUNDS AND FLAVOURS AS CREATIVELY AS YOU CAN.

DREAMING BACK TO THE BAHAMAS ON A WET WELSH AFTERNOON? ASSEMBLE A HAMMOCK AND BLITZ SOME ICE-BLENDED COCKTAILS. WISH YOU WERE NIBBLING STREET FOOD IN PENANG, RATHER THAN STARING AT A LIMP, STORE-BOUGHT SANDWICH? HIT CHINATOWN, ASSEMBLE A PLATTER OF SNACKS, AND DREAM...

COMPLEXITY ✱ ✱ ✱ ✱ ✱

Case study
Carmen Michael, Brazil Enthusiast

I once went to Rio for a one-week holiday but didn't resurface until six months later, when the police apologetically explained that I had outstayed my visa.

Some time later, I'm sitting in a bar, looking for Rio in the unlikely location of George St, Sydney. I down a poorly made caipirinha in which the essential cachaça (sugar-cane whisky) has been sacrilegiously replaced with Bacardi, and talk to Rosina, a Brazilian living in Sydney. She tells me that the place to find Rio in Sydney is Bondi. Bondi!? Having lived there half my life, it didn't fit my image of bohemian Rio...

Nonetheless, on a Saturday morning as I pass under the crumbling arches of the Bondi Beach Pavilion (our own little version of Rio's magnificent Lapa arches) and look down on all the suntanning hedonists below, the differences between Rio and Sydney shrink to the size of a G-string bikini.

I wander past the card players sitting as immoveable as their stone tables, and catch a twang of the Brazilian *berimbou*. The lonely player is Walter, an Italian-Australian who organises Sydney's very own Escola da Samba. The weekend fast becomes a blur of Brazilian travellers, musicians, dancers and students. I meet thrice-divorced and dramatic Syzi and a flirtatious backpacker from São Paulo. I am invited to the Brazilian national day in Marrickville and a rehearsal for Escola da Samba.

I had expected to discover new areas of Sydney but ended up fine-combing my own backyard – now I can only guess at how many other layers of the city are visible to the eye of a traveller rather than that of an indifferent local.

Pros and Cons

+ Improving samba skills
− Sky-high caipirinha standards

Authentic Aims

In *The Art of Travel*, contemporary philosopher Alain de Botton recounts an episode from Joris-Karl Huysman's novel *À Rebours* (1884), in which the central character, the travel-phobic Duc des Esseintes, is inspired to travel to London. Packed, suitably attired and ready to go, he awaits the next train from Paris. While he does so he kills time, enjoying a drink in a wine bar frequented by English expats, before going to an English tavern where he samples a British spread of oxtail soup, smoked haddock, roast beef and potatoes, topped off with ale and a piece of Stilton. When the time comes to leave for London, des Esseintes changes his mind: having enjoyed the 'Englishness' of his experience, he fears the real thing will disappoint. He returns home, never to leave it again.

CARNIVALESQUE FEATHER HEADDRESSES AREN'T STANDARD ATTIRE IN BONDI, THOUGH THEY MIGHT HELP RECAPTURE A RIO VIBE

Same-Name Game

LUSTING OVER A FAR-FLUNG LOCATION? FIND
SOMEWHERE NEARBY THAT SHARES ITS NAME FOR
A TRIP THAT'S SAME SAME, BUT DIFFERENT...

What you'll need

NOSTALGIA FOR A FARAWAY PLACE

Instructions

1. PICK A PLACE YOU'RE LONGING TO REVISIT, SUCH AS YOUR CHILDHOOD HOMETOWN, THE CITY YOU STUDIED IN, OR THE LOCATION OF YOUR WEDDING.

2. NOW HUNT OUT A PLACE CLOSE TO HOME THAT SHARES ITS NAME. SOME CITIES HAVE NAME TWINS (SYDNEY IN CANADA, AND HALF A DOZEN AMERICAN MADRIDS) BUT YOU'LL HAVE MORE LUCK WITH NEIGHBOURHOOD OR STREET NAMES.

3. USE CREATIVE LICENCE WITH SPELLING AND PRONUNCIATION. AN AFTERNOON SEEKING AUCKLAND (NEW ZEALAND) IN OAKLAND (USA) IS PERFECTLY ACCEPTABLE.

4. DON'T LEAVE WITHOUT TAKING A SELFIE BY A ROAD SIGN BEARING THE PLACE'S NAME, TO SPREAD CONFUSION ON SOCIAL MEDIA.

COMPLEXITY ★ ★ ★ ★ ★

- SAME-NAME GAME -

169

Case study

Tasmin Waby, Curious Anglo-Australian

My children were born in the multicultural working-class neighbourhood of Footscray in Melbourne's inner west before we moved to the UK. I'd always been curious about the origin of 'Footscray' (dubbed Footscrazy by locals) so today we're heading to its namesake Foots Cray, in southeast London.

Two trains and a bus ride later we disembark on Foots Cray High St and stare at a fairly nondescript row of houses, a social club, and the entrance to a soft drink factory. We are utterly underwhelmed. 'There has to be more than this!' cries the younger child.

I ask a solitary dog-walker and she directs us to Foots Cray Meadows. 'Sounds promising,' I whisper as soon as we're out of earshot. It delivers in spades. Off the main road we find a 240-acre parkland intersected by the crystal clear River Cray.

A grassy path takes us to a picturesque stone footbridge. I wasn't expecting that when we got off the bus half an hour earlier! The path follows the river through an estate of meadows bounded by cedar trees alive with bird song. This is very different to the gritty metropolis that is 'our Footscray'. We arrive at the heritage-listed Five Arch Bridge, built with bricks in 1781 – before the First Fleet arrived Down Under.

We cap off our adventure with a potter around the slightly dishevelled cemetery next to the All Saints Church on the way back to the bus stop. I later find out this was originally the site of a wooden Saxon Church founded by St Paulinus in the 600s. Our urban adventure turned into quite the history lesson – and our understanding of Foots Cray ran a whole lot deeper.

Pros and Cons

+ Historical learning
− Pangs of yearning

EVEN BLEAK MONUMENTS TO
A DIVIDED PAST, LIKE THE
BERLIN WALL, ELICIT PANGS
OF NOSTALGIA FOR SOME...
REMINISCE WITH CAUTION

Bittersweet Berlin

Nostalgia for the 'good old days' can often be the selective imagining of a mis-remembered past. When the Berlin Wall came tumbling down in 1989, the world was euphoric; the Cold War was finally over. But after the joyous reunification of Germany in 1990, reality settled in – like a hangover after a New Year's Eve party. The wealth of the West failed to lift the former Socialist zone from its economic woes, social services were cut and resentments grew. Some Easterners – or 'Ossies' as they are known in Germany – became disillusioned with the new regime. Nostalgia for the old days – or 'ostalgia' – was on the rise. This curious, bitter-sweet emotion is neatly realised in the cult film *Goodbye Lenin*. It tells the story of a son who goes to extraordinary lengths to prevent his mother from learning that the Berlin Wall has fallen.

BUCOLIC FOOTS CRAY
MEADOWS IN KENT, A
CONTRAST TO GRITTY
FOOTSCRAY IN MELBOURNE,
AUSTRALIA

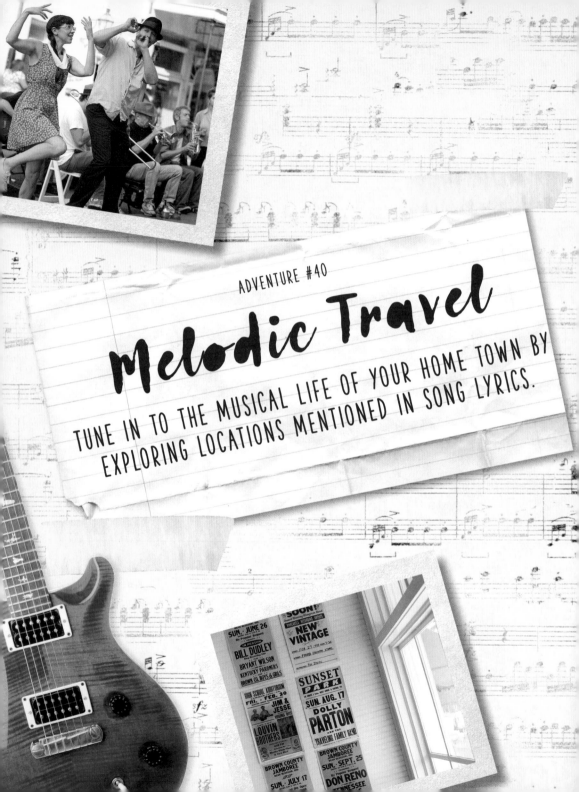

ADVENTURE #40

Melodic Travel

TUNE IN TO THE MUSICAL LIFE OF YOUR HOME TOWN BY EXPLORING LOCATIONS MENTIONED IN SONG LYRICS.

What you'll need

A SONG IN YOUR HEART

LOCAL MUSICAL HISTORY

Instructions

1. BUILD A DAY AROUND LOCATIONS MENTIONED IN SONGS. IT'S A CINCH IF YOU HAVE ACCESS TO NASHVILLE'S COUNTRY MUSIC SCENE, GRUNGE HAUNTS IN SEATTLE, OR MANCHESTER SIGHTS ALLUDED TO IN THE SMITHS' LYRICS.

2. ALTERNATIVELY, WHO'S THE MOST FAMOUS MUSICIAN TO GROW UP IN YOUR TOWN? LISTEN TO THEIR TUNES WHILE TOURING THE STREETS THEY GREW UP IN.

3. IF YOUR TOWN IS NAMECHECKED IN A FEW DIFFERENT SONGS, TAP INTO THE CONTRASTS: HOW DOES THE SQUALID AMSTERDAM OF FRANCOPHONE CHANTEUR JACQUES BREL COMPARE WITH CROWDED HOUSE'S SONG OF THE SAME NAME?

COMPLEXITY ✱ ✱ ✱ ✱ ✱

Case study
Oda O'Carroll, Dubliner & Bad Historian

'Says my oul wan to your oul wan will you come to the Waxies Dargle'... So the raucous 19th-century Dublin pub song recorded by the Pogues starts. But what was a Waxies' Dargle? All I know is it's about an annual day out for cobblers – nowadays that would be a very small party.

I set off on a balmy June afternoon to Irishtown, where the song is based. Stopping outside a bar, I ask an elderly gent about the song. He doesn't know it but says the barman will. Not so. The bemused barman refers me to a group of dockers enjoying pints. They don't either but ask me for a song. A man pushing a buggy, three more walkers and a shopkeeper who has lived in Irishtown all his life all claim ignorance.

I'm enjoying the sunny stroll in a new area and begin to think finding the source of the song is almost incidental. Then bingo, I spot a pub called The Merry Cobbler. This must be associated with the song. I have some top-notch food and an iced drink, waiting for the owner to come over. His local knowledge is plentiful and entertaining; the song describes a special day out for 'waxies' or cobblers, so called as they used wax to waterproof stitching. Unable to stump up the fare to the posh River Dargle further south, a closer seaside suburb, Irishtown, became the 'Waxies' Dargle'.

There's a nearby plaque commemorating the picnic spot no longer at the water's edge, the land between it and the sea having since been reclaimed, he says. I wander and eventually stumble upon an engraved stone on an underwhelming patch of grass. 'Is this it?' I think, surprised. Yes. Surprise is the valuable purpose of any adventure.

Pros and Cons

+ Friendly 'Old Dublin'
+ Unexpected learnings
- Deflating discoveries

CHANNEL THE GENIUS OF A
HOMEGROWN MUSICIAN BY
TOURING THEIR LOCAL HANGOUTS

Rock Star Relics

Some pilgrims kneel at the altars not of saints, but saintly songwriters and godlike guitarists. Graceland draws Elvis devotees, the 'Imagine' mosaic in NYC's Central Park is an essential photo op for Beatles' fans, and humbler memorials honour musicians across genres. If you see cars slowing down in Ljungby, Sweden, they may be seeking a roadside memorial to Metallica's Cliff Burton, near where the bass player died when the band's tour bus skidded off the road. Meanwhile Jim Morrison, ill-fated singer of The Doors, continues rock 'n' roll excesses well beyond his earthly life. Morrison lies buried in Paris' Père LaChaise Cemetery. Alongside bouquets, fans leave bottles of whiskey and packets of cigarettes, and leave feverish love notes next to his tomb.

THE WAXIES' DARGLE:
HONOURED MERRILY
IN SONG, BUT HUMBLY
MEMORIALISED IN SITU...

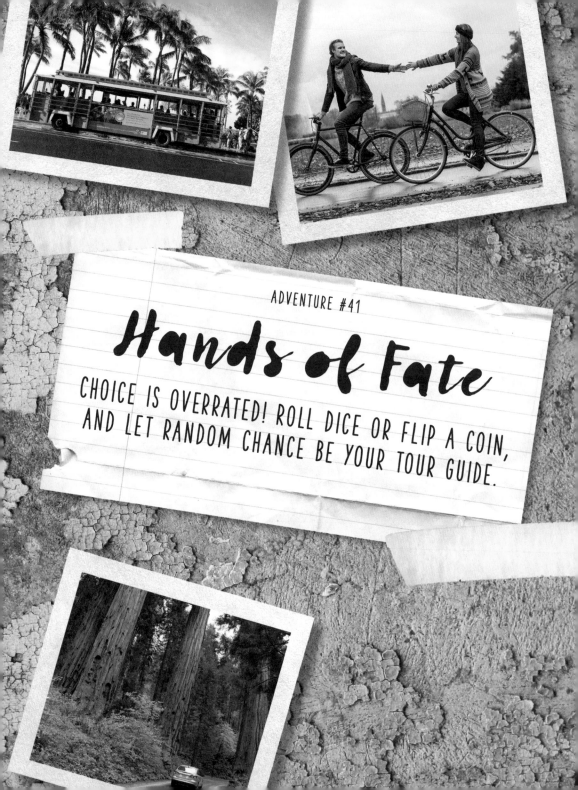

ADVENTURE #41

Hands of Fate

CHOICE IS OVERRATED! ROLL DICE OR FLIP A COIN, AND LET RANDOM CHANCE BE YOUR TOUR GUIDE.

What you'll need

DICE OR A COIN

A TRAVEL BUDDY

A LITTLE-ROAMED NEIGHBOURHOOD

Instructions

RELINQUISH CONTROL TO THE VAGARIES OF RANDOM CHANCE BY WALKING, CYCLING OR DRIVING WHEREVER THIS GAME DEMANDS. THIS ADVENTURE IS MOST FUN WITH A COMPANION (AND THEY'LL MAKE SURE YOU OBEY THE RULES).

START ON YOUR OWN DOORSTEP, FLIPPING A COIN OR ROLLING DICE UNTIL YOU'VE REACHED AN UNEXPECTED LOCATION. IF USING A COIN, DESIGNATE HEADS AS LEFT AND TAILS AS RIGHT. IF YOU HAVE DICE, DECIDE BEFORE ROLLING WHAT THE OUTCOME DICTATES. FOR EXAMPLE, YOUR SCORE MIGHT INDICATE THE NUMBER OF STREETS YOU HAVE TO PASS BEFORE TURNING LEFT (EVEN NUMBER) OR RIGHT (ODD NUMBER).

COMPLEXITY ★ ★ ☆ ☆ ☆

Case study
James Broad, Fateful Traveller

One Friday evening a friend and I arrange to meet at Harrods to see the ridiculously cute animals in the pet shop. To our dismay, the pet department is closed so we are left with no plans and a whole evening to kill. We stand aimlessly on Knightsbridge, neither of us knowing which way to go.

I produce some change from my pocket and suggest that we make a decision based on the flip of a coin.

Heads is established as left and tails as right. This works as a basic rule, but when the first junction approaches we soon need to create more guidelines.

In the space of a few hours we discover a part of London we've never visited before, filled with backstreet pubs and cafes, squares and parks. These days city living is very much about chrome bars and gastro pubs, so it's good to find good old boozers in a part of town that's not known for its down-to-earthness.

Having said that, our final destination is a snobby bar on the King's Road. But when you travel by the coin that's just what may or may not happen.

I'm probably the first person in 20 years to produce change from his pocket rather than plastic in Knightsbridge, but I wouldn't advise flipping an American Express card – they can be a nightmare under windy conditions.

Pros and Cons

+ Sense of abandon
− Coin-flipping dexterity required

Traveller's Roulette

WHY DELIBERATE OVER YOUR DESTINATION? IT'S MUCH MORE FUN TO TAKE THE MIDNIGHT TRAIN GOING ANYWHERE...

What you'll need

TRAIN OR BUS STATION

SENSE OF DESTINY

Instructions

MAKE YOUR WAY TO A TRAIN OR BUS STATION. FROM HERE YOU WILL SET OUT TO A DESTINATION CHOSEN BY 'TRAVELLER'S ROULETTE'. POSSIBLE METHODS INCLUDE:

WITH YOUR BACK TO THE DEPARTURES BOARD, THINK OF A NUMBER BETWEEN ONE AND 10. IF IT'S FIVE, TURN AROUND AND STEP ONTO THE FIFTH BUS OR TRAIN LISTED ON THE BOARD.

WHEN'S YOUR BIRTHDAY? IF IT'S THE 11TH DAY OF THE THIRD MONTH, BOARD A BUS OR TRAIN DEPARTING AT 11 MINUTES PAST THE HOUR, AND DISEMBARK AT THE THIRD STOP.

COMPLEXITY ★ ★ ☆ ☆ ☆

Case study
Nana Luckham, Long-term Londoner

Whenever I'm at the airport, I imagine choosing a destination at random and hopping on a plane. So why not do something similar on a smaller scale? I love to drone on about all London has to offer, but in reality seldom venture outside my home patch. In the spirit of exploration, therefore, I head for my local train station, use my phone to arbitrarily generate a number between 1 and 25 (the number of destinations on offer) and find myself heading for Canada Water, in London's Docklands.

I've changed trains at Canada Water many times, but I've never been above ground. And while hordes of commuters pour down the escalators into the underground system, it's only little me heading for the exit. Once outside I see a bus station, apartment blocks, and, shimmering in the distance, a mid-sized shopping mall. So far, so blah.

Then I spot a striking local library: small, angular and clad in bronzed aluminium. Inside, a spiral wood staircase entices visitors upstairs, where black-and-white prints detail the history of the docks. Downstairs, a buzzy cafe overlooks a small lake. This, it appears, is the Canada Water, which I learn is the only freshwater body in the Docklands. It's named after the former Canada Dock, which was used by ships from – you guessed it – Canada. There are ducks, a fishing pontoon, and it's framed by a massive outdoor gear store. If I ever need to buy an inflatable canoe, I know where to come.

Heading south through a concrete blot of an entertainment complex, I spot a small Vietnamese restaurant called Cafe East. It's surprisingly full for 11.45 am on a Wednesday, so I decide to settle down for some *bun cha*. Who knew that a cafe overlooking a car park in south London was the place to come for an authentic taste of Hanoi?

Pros and Cons

+ Escaping one's rut
- Desire to return to one's rut

Unplanned Capers

Even without any desire to randomise their destination, a number of travellers have embarked on journeys wholly different to the ones they planned. In 2014, British holidaymaker Kevin Jones booked bargain flights from Birmingham, UK to Trinidad, discovering upon arrival at the West Midlands airport that his seat was on a plane departing from Birmingham, Alabama. While this misfortune was halted at the check-in desk, in 2015 traveller Jeff Waldman boarded a plane to the wrong destination, arriving in Dallas despite flashing a Los Angeles ticket. Even more of a shock was experienced by Dutch student Milan Schipper in 2017. Bound for the sun-kissed Aussie east coast, Schipper found himself battling a snowstorm, having accidentally booked his ticket to Sydney, Canada.

NO MORE DECISION FATIGUE: SELECT A DESTINATION AT RANDOM OR BOARD A BUS CHOSEN BY ITS FLASHY DECOR

Alternating Travel

THE ROAD LESS TRAVELLED IS ONLY A FEW STEPS FROM YOUR FRONT DOOR. FOLLOW ALTERNATING TRAVEL DIRECTIONS FOR A RANDOM AND REVEALING WALK AROUND YOUR NEIGHBOURHOOD.

What you'll need

A SPARE AFTERNOON

THE ABILITY TO TELL LEFT FROM RIGHT

Instructions

THE RULES ARE SIMPLE: TAKE A RIGHT TURN AS YOU LEAVE YOUR FRONT DOOR, THEN A LEFT, THEN A RIGHT, ALTERNATING THE DIRECTIONS UNTIL YOU'RE ENJOYABLY LOST. THE GOAL IS TO ZIG-ZAG YOUR WAY THROUGH ROADS THAT YOU MAY HAVE OVERLOOKED. PERHAPS YOU'LL MEANDER AMONG RESIDENTIAL STREETS, OR MAYBE YOU'LL STUMBLE ON A FASCINATING STATUE, IDYLLIC PARK OR TREE-LINED LANE YOU'VE NEVER NOTICED.

CONTINUE ALTERNATING UNTIL SOMETHING BLOCKS YOUR PATH, SUCH AS A LAKE OR BUILDING SITE - OR UNTIL YOU FIND SOMEWHERE YOU CAN'T RESIST LINGERING...

COMPLEXITY ★ ★ ★ ★ ★

187

Case study
Etain O'Carroll, Suburban Stroller

Oxford, the city of dreaming spires and the academic elite, is very divided: there's virtually no interaction between town and gown. I live in one of those strange places where a single road divides two very different communities – one side has nice houses, cars and lots of extensions going up; on the other side there's a run-down council estate.

Right: cherry blossom petals fall through the air like slow snowflakes. The idyllic scene is shattered when I take my first right and see two learner drivers about to collide. I'm deep in the heart of suburbia. Two men chat over a wall, one giant belly hidden from the other by the concrete garden wall.

Left: around the next corner a granny is dropped off after a lazy lunch. Her son waves goodbye and she waddles into her house, her lurid orange sunglasses matching the wholly unnatural colour of her hair. Another learner driver does the slowest three-point turn imaginable. There's oceans of room on either side but he's going nowhere.

Right: I turn into a graffiti-clad laneway and emerge on the main road. A child is teasing a Rottweiler in an untended garden strewn with dandelions.

Left: I'm cruising the council estate, no idea where I'm going but knowing exactly how to get there. A kid on a scooter flashes past with a walkie-talkie pinned across his chest.

Right: I turn into another quiet but run-down residential street. Potholes litter the tarmac, and a massive pink armchair lords it over the scene, weathered by rain and wind and covered in old tyres. Like most people, I tend to take the same route to and from work or the shops. I realise how easy it is to avoid swathes of your immediate surroundings.

Pros and Cons

+ Meditative walking pace
– Disorientation

IF YOU'RE ACCUSTOMED TO
STROLLING THE SAME PATHS TO
AND FROM HOME, THERE MAY BE
MYSTERIES YOU'RE MISSING...

The Divided Brain

The right side of the brain is primarily concerned with the emotions and recognition of shapes and topographical forms. The left is devoted to logical, communicative skills such as writing (if you're right-handed) and language and numerical comprehension. The two distinct areas are joined by the corpus callosum. If you ever find yourself weighing the pros and cons of a decision, and choosing between two opposing viewpoints, that's because you are. According to some neurological theorists, decisions require the brain to take a straw poll between the two sides, both of which offer different, sometimes incompatible, opinions. If someone suffers a brain injury that damages the corpus callosum and separates the two sides, and that person is still living, you can potentially trick that person's brain into allowing you to converse with its two distinct sides.

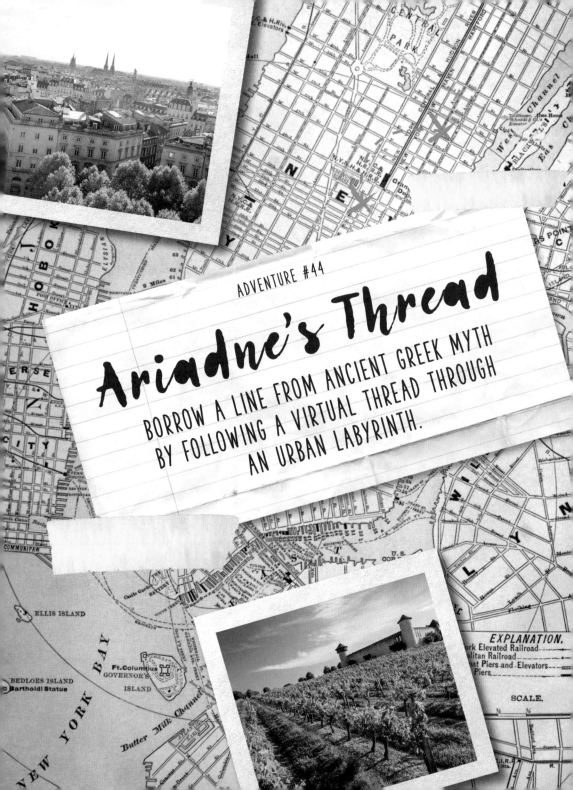

Ariadne's Thread

BORROW A LINE FROM ANCIENT GREEK MYTH BY FOLLOWING A VIRTUAL THREAD THROUGH AN URBAN LABYRINTH.

What you'll need

AN 'ARIADNE'

ONLINE OR PAPER MAP

Instructions

1. SELECT YOUR 'ARIADNE', WHOSE FAVOURITE PLACES WILL DICTATE YOUR JOURNEY. S/HE COULD BE A FRIEND, FRIEND OF A FRIEND, OR SOMEONE YOU FIND BY DIALLING A RANDOM PHONE NUMBER.

2. ASK YOUR 'ARIADNE' FOR THEIR SIX FAVOURITE PLACES IN THE CITY.

3. PLOT THESE SIX PLACES ON A CITY MAP AND DEVISE A ROUTE CONNECTING ALL OF THEM. THIS ROUTE IS THE 'ARIADNE'S THREAD' YOU MUST FOLLOW THROUGH THE URBAN MAZE.

4. FOLLOW THE ROUTE, STOPPING AT ARIADNE'S FAVOURITE LOCATIONS AND DISCOVERING YOUR OWN ALONG THE WAY.

COMPLEXITY ✱ ✱ ✱ ✱ ✱

Case study
Joël Henry, Enigma Chaser

I begin my experiment by asking around to see if anybody knows of an Ariadne. A friend of a friend vaguely knows one who lives in Bordeaux and gives me her email address. I send her an email telling her about the Ariadne's Thread experiment and ask if she'd be kind enough to send me a list of her favourite places in the city. She replies:

'Having considered your Ariadne's Thread at some length, I invite you to visit the Bordeaux of my first times: the first time I made love; the first time I was paid; the first time I drank whisky; the first time I was in a fight; the first time I had my own address; the first time I saw the Tour de France go by.

'In no particular order, these places are: 87 Rue Emile Fourcand; the Bar de la Marine; the city football stadium; in the shadow of the Mission Haut-Brion water tower; the Galerie Bordelaise; the Café Français.'

Although she is corporeally absent, Ariadne haunts me throughout the course of my journey. Visiting the places in the order she suggested, I can't help asking myself which particular first time they might have staged.

One would expect that it was at the city stadium she first saw the Tour de France. Similarly, 87 Rue Emile Fourcand would probably have been her first address. That fisticuffs might have been thrown under the turn-of-the-century cover of the Galerie Bordelaise was within the realms of possibility. But had she been a waitress at the Bar de la Marine or the Café Français? And what had she been up to under that water tower…

Pros and Cons

✛ Walking in a stranger's shoes
– Unanswered questions

PONT DE PIERRE IN BORDEAUX
IS LADEN WITH TWINKLING
LIGHTS THAT SEEM TO WHISPER
'EXPLORE ME'

Minotaur Myth

According to myth, Ariadne is the daughter of Crete's King Minos, the guardian of the labyrinth-dwelling, half-man, half-bull Minotaur. Every nine years, seven unlucky Athenian girls and boys are sent to Crete to be sacrificed to this beast. The noble Theseus volunteers to be among the sacrificial group, determined to beat the Minotaur. Upon seeing the hunky Theseus, Ariadne slips him a thread, which he fastens to the entrance of the labyrinth. He finds and kills the Minotaur and, thanks to Ariadne's thread, emerges to claim victory – and the girl. Alas, owing to an unfortunate storm, or perhaps a god-induced lapse of memory, Theseus abandons poor Ariadne on an island. She is eventually rescued by Dionysus, party guy of wine, women and ecstasy, whom she marries.

YOUR OWN ARIADNE'S
THREAD NEED NOT
INVOLVE VANQUISHING
BEASTS OR A SKIMPY
WARRIOR COSTUME

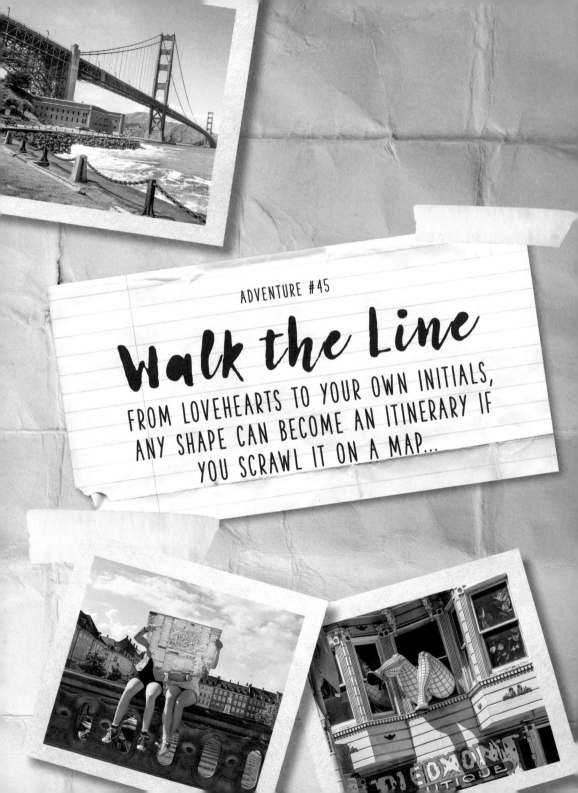

ADVENTURE #45

Walk the Line

FROM LOVEHEARTS TO YOUR OWN INITIALS,
ANY SHAPE CAN BECOME AN ITINERARY IF
YOU SCRAWL IT ON A MAP...

What you'll need

MAP OF YOUR TOWN OR REGION

COLOURED PEN

MEANS OF TRANSPORT

Instructions

POWER DOWN ANY ONLINE MAPS, THIS ADVENTURE REQUIRES A PAPER MAP ONLY.

WITH A COLOURED PEN, DOODLE A FLOWING LINE ONTO YOUR MAP. IT COULD BE YOUR INITIALS IN CURSIVE SCRIPT, A NONSENSICAL SCRIBBLE, OR SOMETHING A LITTLE MORE (AHEM) SENSUOUS. THIS SHAPE IS YOUR ROUTE; FOLLOW IT AS CLOSELY AS YOU CAN.

COMPLEXITY ★ ★ ★ ★ ★

195

Case study

Don George,
Heart-Stopping Travel Writer

Hearts and San Francisco go together. So I take a red pen to a map of the city and trace a sloping heart shape any child would be proud of: my itinerary.

At the ferry building on San Francisco Bay, the smell of the sea wafts over the first lunch patrons. Two sleek men clink glasses of champagne. 'To San Francisco,' one says. 'To us,' the other smiles. I cross under the balmy palms of the Embarcadero, but then encounter my first challenge: heart lines don't follow street lines. I step inside a building, only to be swept into a swirling sea of blue suits, name tags and health products. A silky woman strokes my arm and smiles. 'Would you like to sample our latest skin enhancer?'

My heartline leads me inexorably down a tight, garbage-scented alley where I squeeze past a parked SUV. Inside I glimpse long stockinged legs and two torsos crushed in embrace. I duck through a service exit and emerge opposite the Bureau of Citizenship and Immigration Services. A monk in flowing robes and a young woman queue patiently.

The trail beats on, past the metal-fenced tennis courts of the Golden Gateway Club, where a yellow ball sails over the fence and bounces right into the delighted hands of a pink-dressed Asian girl. 'Love-forty,' a man shouts as the girl throws the ball into the air.

My itinerary ends at Yin and Yang by Robert Arneson. I sit by this artwork and think about all the veins of yin and yang in the body of mankind. In a patch of grass behind the Arneson, a man spreads a blanket for his lover, and their fingers intertwine: heart-lines.

Pros and Cons

+ Urban obstacle course
– Inability to walk through walls

TREAT YOUR CITY LIKE AN
OBSTACLE COURSE BY FOLLOWING
A ROUTE DRAWN FREEHAND ON
YOUR MAP

FREE YOURSELF FROM
DEPENDENCE ON ONLINE
MAPS BY FAITHFULLY
FOLLOWING A DOODLE
DRAWN ON A PAPER MAP

Epic Artworks

Following your line around the city is akin to creating invisible graffiti. It would be difficult to beat Hugh Pryor and Jeremy Wood, who decided to answer the question 'What's the world's biggest "IF"?' by drawing one in southern England. Their 'IF' incorporated the destinations of Iffley, Iford, Ifield and Ifold. The resulting itinerary, which they 'drew' by car, was 863km long – the equivalent font size would be 319,334,400 points – and took a total of two days and six hours to complete. You may be more inspired by the enormous urban creations of Christo and Jeanne-Claude. The Bulgarian-Moroccan modern art duo gift-wrapped the Reichstag in Berlin, as well as Paris' Pont-Neuf, and installed 37km of orange-hued gates in New York City's Central Park.

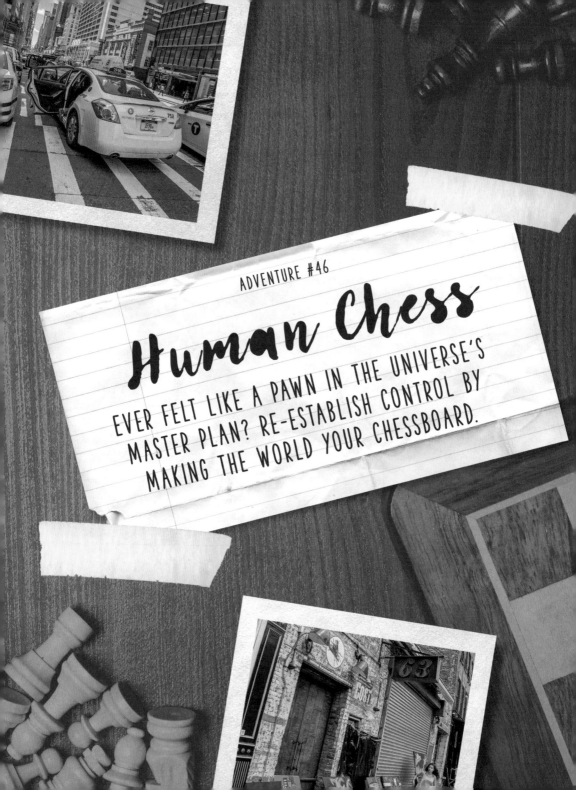

ADVENTURE #46

Human Chess

EVER FELT LIKE A PAWN IN THE UNIVERSE'S MASTER PLAN? RE-ESTABLISH CONTROL BY MAKING THE WORLD YOUR CHESSBOARD.

What you'll need

ORGANISATIONAL SKILLS

WILLING PLAYERS

COSTUMES (BLACK AND WHITE T-SHIRTS WILL DO)

Instructions

TRANSFORM AN ENTIRE NEIGHBOURHOOD INTO A BOARD GAME. FIND A PART OF YOUR CITY THAT HAS A GRID-LIKE STREET LAYOUT AND YOU CAN PLAY ANYTHING FROM CHESS TO CHECKERS.

REMEMBER, YOU DON'T NEED AN ENORMOUS CAST OF CHARACTERS TO FILL ALL POSITIONS. PLAYERS CAN BE REASSIGNED TO NEW ROLES WHEN THEY ARE KILLED OR CAPTURED.

HUMAN BOARD GAMES ARE TIRING, THIRSTY WORK, SO ENSURE YOUR BOARD-GAME LOCATION IS CLOSE TO A WATERING HOLE OR TWO.

COMPLEXITY ★ ★ ★ ★ ★

Case study
Sharilyn Neidhardt, Human Chess Pro

Orchestrating human chess is a massive organisational effort. I spend the three weeks before each game posting to online bulletin boards, sending emails and attempting to assign the roles to volunteers. I also select a neighbourhood and design the game board. I get in touch with local papers as well as coffee shops, bars and other businesses in the area to call their attention to what we are doing.

Even if I don't get all 32 pieces covered by volunteers, we play the game anyway. I've managed to fill every single piece on the board only once, and that was the first game I organised, on Manhattan's Lower East Side. The game is operated from a nominated home base, usually a park.

Two players – usually me and another person – play a chess game on a regular board. Following each move, we use a mobile phone to call each human chess piece and tell them what to do. Each human chess piece has a map of the neighbourhood showing which intersection corresponds to which square. When I call the white bishop (for example) and tell her to move to B5, she can look on her map and see that she needs to walk to the corner of South Fifth and Bedford Ave. During the endgame, we start funnelling captured pieces to a social venue, usually a bar somewhere on the game board.

Human chess is more interesting for the pieces than the controllers, for whom the game is not so different from any other one. One knight described his experience thus: 'An attractive woman walks by. One of the Bishops wonders if she is interested in chess. If so, I wonder if she has ever had any fantasies about the Black Knight? Both Bishops express regret that they are men of the cloth.'

Pros and Cons

+ Surreal sociability
− Organisational effort

Pawn Stars

Tip your hat to Ivan Nikolić and Goran Arsović, who played the world's longest ever game of chess in Belgrade in 1989. Frustratingly there was no nail-biting finish to this 269-move, 20-hour marathon: the match ended in a draw. Chess' snail's-pace reputation has made the game ripe for reinvention. Dadaist artist Marcel Duchamp (best known for his upturned urinal artwork, *Fountain*) was challenged to chess by then 20-year-old writer and hedonist Eve Babitz...who insisted on playing him in the nude. Less blush-inducing is chessboxing, in which players use brain and brawn in alternating chess and boxing matches (concussion permitting). Dutch artist Iepe Rubingh originally conceived of chessboxing as a performance art piece, but the hybrid sport quickly gained a cult following.

CHESS REQUIRES MENTAL GYMNASTICS, SO WHY NOT REWARD YOUR EFFORTS BY PLAYING FROM THE SILKY WATERS OF SZECHENYI BATHS IN BUDAPEST?

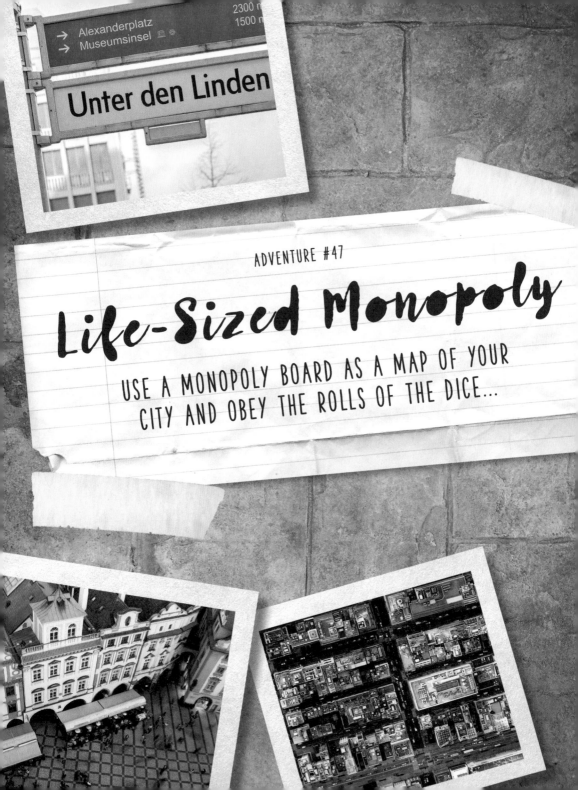

ADVENTURE #47

Life-Sized Monopoly

USE A MONOPOLY BOARD AS A MAP OF YOUR CITY AND OBEY THE ROLLS OF THE DICE...

What you'll need

MONOPOLY BOARD OF YOUR CITY

PAIR OF DICE

FELLOW PLAYERS

Instructions

BOARD GAMING BECOMES LIFE-SIZED ON THIS PERSPECTIVE-ALTERING ADVENTURE.
SEE HOW THE BOARD GAME MONOPOLY MEASURES UP TO REALITY: FOLLOW THE
OFFICIAL RULES OF THE GAME BUT INSTEAD OF MOVING A TOKEN AROUND A
BOARD, MOVE YOURSELF TO EACH DESTINATION. VISIT STREETS AND STATIONS,
AVOID BEING SENT TO JAIL, AND DON'T HOARD THE MONOPOLY MONEY.

COMPLEXITY ★ ★ ★ ★ ★

Case study
Joël Henry, Berlin Boardgamer

Split in two during the Cold War between capitalist West Berlin and Communist East Berlin, Germany's capital was deprived of Monopoly until its reunification in 1990. The official version, now found in every toy shop, follows an urban trajectory from blue-collar Lützowplatz to the ostentatious Ku'damm and Unter den Linden. We throw the dice. Three and five make eight: Kollwitzplatz. Tally-ho!

It's no mean feat navigating one's way about town using only a Monopoly board. Berliners are evidently more used to providing directions with a conventional city map. It takes us the better part of an hour to find Kollwitzplatz, the Aladdin's Cave of the intelligentsia under the Communist regime, and since transformed into Berlin's boho mecca, replete with design-heavy cafes, art galleries and deluxe squats.

One and six: Bahnhof Zoo, where you can find practically anything: showers, newspapers from all over the world, Italian-style espresso, poppyseed bagels and a troupe of Berlin dancers shoehorned into extravagant costumes. Six and three: Alexanderplatz, that paragon of Soviet-era architecture. The statue of Karl Marx still stands.

Two ones: Olympischestrasse. Its proximity to Alexanderplatz on the board should not be taken for geographical neighbourliness. The peaceful avenue, lined with chichi villas and leading to the old Nazi Olympic stadium, is in fact 20km from Alexanderplatz.

Four and two: Go to jail. Do not pass 'Go'. Tegel prison has no visiting hours. The high concrete walls, barbed wire and surveillance cameras dissuade us from attempting to bribe the guards with our thick wads of 10,000 and 50,000 Monopoly Deutschmarks.

Pros and Cons

+ Outdoor adventure
- Jail time

Monopoly Miscellany

Shamelessly capitalistic, Monopoly is a game where it is only possible to win at another's expense; winners live it up in Mayfair, while the losers tough it out on Old Kent Road. Ironically, Monopoly was invented by a poor, unemployed man, Charles B. Darrow of Pennsylvania, during the Depression in 1934. Today the game is licensed to more than 45 countries and appears in 26 different languages. The longest game in history took 70 days to complete. The silliest, longest Monopoly games ever played took 99 hours (in a bathtub), 45 days (underwater) and upside down (36 hours). *Do Not Pass Go*, written by the comedic British writer Tim Moore, charts the history of London by investigating every stop on the board.

BERLIN'S MUSEUM ISLAND: BEST APPROACHED BY BRIDGE, BARGE OR MANOEUVRES ON A MONOPOLY BOARD?

ADVENTURE #48

12 Travel

DECISION-MAKING IS A BORE, SO FIND YOUR
DESTINY BY FOLLOWING LUCKY NUMBER 12...

What you'll need

MINIMAL NUMERICAL APTITUDE

Instructions

RESEARCHING WHEN AND WHERE TO TRAVEL IS TOO TAXING. INSTEAD, LET LUCKY NUMBER 12 BE THE THEME OF AN EXCURSION, INCLUDING IT AS MANY TIMES (AND IN AS MANY DIFFERENT WAYS) AS YOU CAN.

TAKE A TRAIN THAT LEAVES AT 12.12, DISEMBARKING AT THE TWELFTH STOP; OR DRIVE ONLY ALONG HIGHWAY NUMBER 12. ONCE YOU ARRIVE, WALK 12 BLOCKS, FIND A LUNCH COSTING £1.20 OR £12, AND VISIT THE TWELFTH MOST POPULAR ATTRACTION IN TOWN (HEY, SOMEONE'S GOT TO).

FIND A HOTEL AND REQUEST TO STAY IN ROOM NUMBER 12, AND ORDER THE TWELFTH ITEM ON THE ROOM SERVICE MENU.

COMPLEXITY ★ ★ ★ ★ ☆

Case study
Michael Clerizo,
Dodecaphonous Discoverer

'Twelve Travel' is inspired by 'dodecaphony', the 12-tone method of musical composition developed by composer Arnold Schönberg. And 12 can be a difficult number – I know, because I phoned National Rail enquiries and asked them to find me 'a train that leaves a station at 12 minutes after any hour'.

Walking through my local station, a poster declares, 'Trains depart every 12 minutes' from Mill Hill East on the Northern Line. Twelve stops after Mill Hill East is Moorgate, and disappointment. Stockbrokers and money managers are fine but the streetscape is boring. Every façade has been designed by consultancies that follow orthodoxy masquerading as creativity.

I decide to improvise, and head back to the Northern Line. Twelve stops south of Moorgate is the quaintly named Tooting Bec. I feel quietly confident in saying that there has never been a design consultant anywhere near Tooting Bec. The suburb is full of small businesses that unselfconsciously mark out their territory.

The Café Espresso boasts 'hot and cold meals cooked to the highest standards'. At the local Asian centre a sign announces that the vegetarian lunch club meets every day; the nonvegetarian club meets only on Saturdays. Holy Trinity parish has a one-page history stating that 'there is little in the way of outstanding historical events'.

Returning to the station, I pass a piano on the pavement. I play a few bars of 'Good Golly Miss Molly'. It isn't up to Schönberg's standard, but no one seems to mind.

Pros and Cons

+ Excuse for eccentricity

– Uninspiring results

Magic Of 12

'Dodecaphony' or serial music is the 12-tone method of musical composition developed by the controversial Austrian composer Arnold Schönberg (1874–1951). When Schönberg abandoned tonality in favour of his mathematical technique (which might be described as 'composition with constraints'), he did to music what the Cubist painters did to perspective – and was received with similar levels of popularity.

Schönberg was one of the most influential composers of modern times, but his work was rarely performed in his lifetime and was continuously attacked by critics, many of whom had never even heard it. Interestingly enough, Schönberg is said to have suffered from fear of the number 13 (triskaidekaphobia).

IS IT A LONDON
UNDERGROUND LOGO, OR
A TOTEM DRAWING YOU
TOWARDS YOUR TRAVEL
DESTINY?

Expedition to K2

FOLLOW THE FOOTSTEPS OF K2'S BRAVE CONQUERORS...
THOUGH YOUR JOURNEY TAKES YOU TO THE MAP
GRID-REFERENCE, NOT THE MOUNTAIN.

What you'll need

PAPER ATLAS OF YOUR CITY

BICYCLE OR CAR (DEPENDING ON THE EXPEDITION'S SCALE)

Instructions

1. OPEN YOUR ATLAS AT RANDOM AND FIND THE GRID-REFERENCE K2 ON THAT PAGE.

2. HIKE, BIKE OR DRIVE TO THAT LOCATION AND EXPLORE THE AREA, WITH THE SAME DILIGENCE AND CARE OF A MOUNTAINEER REACHING AN UNCONQUERED PEAK.

3. IF K2 LEADS YOU TO WATER OR INHOSPITABLE DESERT, YOU ARE HEREBY PERMITTED TO FLIP TO ANOTHER RANDOM PAGE AND TRY AGAIN. HOWEVER, 'BORING' AND 'NOTHING TO DO THERE' ARE NOT EXCUSES TO DO SO.

COMPLEXITY ★ ★ ☆ ☆ ☆

Case study
Kachael Antony, Suburban Voyager

Compared to the fearsome challenges of scaling K2 in the Karakoram range, exploring the region of K2 on Map 531 in a Melbourne street directory is arguably easier, being both frostbite and sherpa free.

Eschewing the temptation of a seaside stroll (F12) or a visit to the Air Museum (L5), I finally set foot on K2, only to discover that it is pouring with rain. Though pelted with rain and bullied by the winds, I remain grimly determined to enjoy K2 to the full – namely, the Cheltenham-Moorabbin Returned Servicemen's League Club, tastefully positioned by Kingston Heath Reserve, a suburban slice of greenery fronting the highway. I set about photographing the war memorials one invariably finds at an Australian RSL.

Seeking to escape the elements, I venture indoors to sample the gastronomic offerings therein and find myself surrounded by snowy-haired senior citizens, a good number of whom are sporting walking frames. Deciding against the sweets and cakes on offer (which appear to have been 'assembled' rather than 'cooked'), I opt instead for a plain coffee, whereupon I am directed to a coffee machine in the gaming room. Having sought instruction on its usage I sit down to sample my hot beverage while all around me pensioners plunge their savings, coin by coin, into the 'one armed bandits' (aka poker machines).

Finding the atmosphere somewhat depressing, and the coffee entirely undrinkable, I take a short stroll around K2. I pause to photograph a large fibreglass tyrannosaurus rex on display at a garden shop amid children's swing sets and garden gnomes, and then head home. While the snowy mists of far-off K2 remain a mystery to me, they can surely be no stranger than the flat plains of deepest suburbia.

Pros and Cons

+ Broad definition of 'expedition'
- Bleak suburbs
- Bland food

ADVENTURE #50

Out of Office

SO YOUR OFFICE IS STIFLING AND YOUR CO-WORKERS UNHINGED? SNOOP AROUND SOMEONE ELSE'S WORKPLACE INSTEAD.

What you'll need

SMART CLOTHING

TAKEAWAY COFFEE

PALPABLE AIR OF DEFEAT

RED TAPE (OPTIONAL)

Instructions

FOR AN EASY VERSION OF THIS ADVENTURE, ASK AN EMPLOYED FRIEND TO SNEAK YOU INTO THEIR OFFICE AND GIVE YOU A QUICK TOUR...BEFORE LEAVING YOU TO SPIN IN OFFICE CHAIRS, RANSACK THE STATIONERY CUPBOARD OR GATECRASH A MEETING, ARMED WITH A LATTE-TO-GO AND A FEW BUZZWORDS.

IF YOU'RE FEELING BOLD, BLEND IN AT A RANDOM OFFICE. IN TIMES OF TIGHT SECURITY, PREPARE TO BE TURNED ON YOUR HEEL. BUT SUITABLE COVER STORIES MIGHT INCLUDE BEING EARLY FOR A JOB INTERVIEW OR HAVING A MEETING WITH CAROL FROM HR (THERE'S ALWAYS A CAROL FROM HR).

COMPLEXITY ★ ★ ★ ★ ★

Case study
Joël Henry, Office Infiltrator

The CUS is the city's highest authority, from beautification of roundabouts to the constabulary to the philharmonic orchestra. Other than the top storey – the site of the mayor's office, guarded by a touchy receptionist – nobody pays the slightest attention as you wander through the corridors. I sink into an armchair in the lobby and spend an hour devouring the assorted free magazines and prospectuses fanned out on a counter.

Noon's approach brings my mind to thoughts of lunch. To be served in the canteen, I have to convince the member of staff queuing in front of me to pay for my lunch on his swipe card, in exchange for cash. It costs a mere €3.19 for a delicious salmon and fennel roll, a chocolate mousse and a small pitcher of white wine – to the astonishment of my neighbours, who inform me that alcohol consumption by staff at lunch time is frowned upon.

But I am on holiday, a fact I am unable to hide for long. Instead of tut-tutting, my dining companions list their favourite haunts in the building: a small flowered patio that's favourably disposed to meditative reflection, the gallery of abstract paintings that hangs on the walls of the council chambers, the municipal print room for its casual ambience and intoxicating fumes...

I swing an invitation to an office, that of Mrs H., a bubbly young woman in charge of the roads department. She patiently explains the laborious procedure required to name a new street. I confess my fantasy of doing her job, voluntarily, for an hour or two, as the zenith of this travel experience. She considers my request before concluding, with sincere regret, 'The thing is, there's nothing to do today.'

Pros and Cons

+ Fly-on-the-wall insights
– Urge for photocopier mischief

MONOCHROME MONOTONY OR
A PLAYGROUND FOR CREATIVE
THINKING? SEE HOW YOUR
OFFICE ENVIRONMENT COMPARES

TO FEEL LIKE ONE WORKER
BEE IN A HUMMING
HIVE, STAND AT SHIBUYA
INTERSECTION IN TOKYO,
THOUGHT TO BE THE
BUSIEST IN THE WORLD

Otherworldly Offices

Sneak into the world's most opulent workspaces and it might ruin you for '60s-style concrete blocks forever. Architects are increasingly designing offices to soothe stressed workers with the illusion of wilderness. Office spaces designed by Selgas Cano Architecture have floor-to-ceiling windows overlooking forest; leaves fall softly on the glass roof while natural light floods in. Channelling a more villainous vibe are the creations of Albert France-Lanord Architects. Burrowed 30m underground between granite walls and brooding rock, their White Mountain offices in Stockholm seem a likelier location to brainstorm plans for the apocalypse, rather than pick over end-of-year accounts.

Index
Pick a style for your everyday adventure...

Findings

Findings

Published in July 2018 by Lonely Planet Global Limited
CRN 554153
www.lonelyplanet.com
ISBN 978 1 7870 1358 2
© Lonely Planet 2017
Printed in China
10 9 8 7 6 5 4 3 2 1

Publishing Director Piers Pickard
Associate Publisher Robin Barton
Commissioning Editor Anita Isalska
Proof Reader Yolanda Zapaterra
Art Director Daniel Di Paolo
Designer Lauren Egan
Illustrator Alice Bowsher
Print Production Lisa Ford, Nigel Longuet
Cover images Evgeny Karandaev / Shutterstock, AKaiser / Shutterstock, Marques / Shutterstock, Ints Vikmanis / Getty Images, LordRunar / Getty Images, moneymaker11 / Shutterstock, SombatDL / Shutterstock, QQ7 / Getty Images, f9photos / Shutterstock

Contributors Rachael Antony, James Bainbridge, Louise Bastock, James Broad, Kerry Christiani, Michael Clerizo, Lucy Corne, Joe Davis, Sally Dillon, Belinda Dixon, Don George, Eric Hazard, Carolyn B. Heller, Joël Henry, Virginia Jealous, Lauren Keith, Pat Kinsella, Alex Landrigan, Ali Lemer, Nana Luckham, Marika McAdam, Daniel McCrohan, Carmen Michael, Jeremy Moon, Sharilyn Neidhardt, Karyn Noble, Etain O'Carroll, Oda O'Carroll, Lorna Parkes, Tom Parkinson, David Prater, Sarah Reid, Tim Richards, John A. Vlahides, Tasmin Waby, Luke Waterson, Christina Webb

STAY IN TOUCH lonelyplanet.com/contact

AUSTRALIA The Malt Store, Level 3, 551 Swanston St, Carlton, Victoria 3053 T: 03 8379 8000

IRELAND Digital Depot, Roe Lane (off Thomas St), Digital Hub, Dublin 8, D08 TCV4

USA 124 Linden St, Oakland, CA 94607 T: 510 250 6400

UNITED KINGDOM 240 Blackfriars Rd, London SE1 8NW T: 020 3771 5100

Paper in this book is certified against the Forest Stewardship Council™ standards. FSC™ promotes environmentally responsible, socially beneficial and economically viable management of the world's forests.